MW01242868

12/12/17

The Spanish Dancer

Gene House

Dick and Carol,

Merry Christmas and have
a wonderful New Year

Gene House

Running Quail Press

USA

THE SPANISH DANCER

Running Quail Press, Inc.,
P.O. Box 5274
Peoria, AZ 85385-5274
www.runningquailpress.com

ISBN: 978-0-9862708-6-4

Printed in the United States of America

First Edition

Cover Design by Betts McCalla

Dedication

   This book is dedicated to my mother, Rebeccah House, whose search for our ancestors stirred in me a consuming interest in the genealogy of our family. The big box of her notes, pedigree charts, letters to libraries, cemeteries and government agencies and their answers gave me a real kick in the pants to continue her work. Keep in mind that she did her research before the Internet got started. Learning about our forebears' lives and their accomplishments can stimulate the imagination as it did mine.

Acknowledgments

Linda Perkins, my editor, whose depth of knowledge of how to write creative and interesting pieces, improved my writing immensely. Her long hours and nights working on my manuscript have paid high dividends to improve the story, including alliterations, parallelisms, and dynamics.

Gretchen Logan, my very excellent proofreader, tirelessly marked and re-marked my manuscripts by identifying spelling, sentence construction, and grammatical errors. My creative writing instructor, Michael Crawley, whose remarks made my stories interesting to read.

Also I would like to thank every member of the Ahwatukee Recreation Center (ARC) Writers' Group, particularly Judy Lovins for her insight and keen mind that picked up details and confusions that I completely missed. Ben Wilson's comments inspired me to keep writing fiction. And Sandy Smith, our intrepid leader, who pointed out story-line puzzlements and some lack of logic.

Finally, thank you, Charlie Lanchantin, for reading the finished manuscript cover-to-cover, adding notes, and leaving substantial enhancement comments.

Table of Contents

Chapter One

January 8, 1815

A drop of sweat started down the big pirate's cheek. It caught in the deep groove of the scar that ran from beneath his ear to his chin. The air was cold. The early morning fog lay heavy around them. A gray light had just begun to appear over the swamp to the East. It would be sunup soon. The sweat fell from the pirate's chin as he turned and grinned at William Russell.

"Ye scared, Youngster?" He asked in a heavy cockney accent.

"*Youngster!*" William resented being called that, particularly by someone who was probably only a year or two older. He gripped his long rifle tightly and looked back at the pirate--not sure what to say. This was a shooting fight, and men were going to get hurt and killed. He might be one of them. His palms were damp with perspiration. He tried to dry his hands on his pants. William had heard of the American militia on the left near the swamp, running from their positions on New Year's Day when the British attacked. This knowledge didn't help relieve his fears.

Being afraid was natural. He knew this. The men around him on the battle line had fear, but would they hold and fight? He prayed that he would have the courage to stay with them. He was scared alright. He was scared of the bullets that would be aimed at him, scared of the canons that would be fired at him, but most of all he was afraid of himself. Would he be a coward and run?

Finally, remembering his father's advice, *Always tell the truth,* yet not being able to get the word out, he sheepishly nodded "yes" to the pirate. He shivered in the cold morning air, but there were beads of sweat across his forehead and upper lip.

"Do not ye worry! Tis de waiting dat sets de nerves on edge. Once de fight starts, ye do not have time to think of how frightened ye be. Ye just get into de fight and have at 'em," said the pirate sounding confident.

This mountain of a man beside William had obviously been in more than one shooting scrape. After all, he was one of Jean Lafitte's men and had probably been in pirate raids and ship-to-ship fights. He hadn't gotten that scar just playing around. He looked to be six or seven inches taller than William, who was considered tall for his age at five-foot-eleven inches. The pirate's weight must be about 250 pounds. At his last weighing on the grain scale at Fogerd's Seed Store back home, William had barely reached 170 pounds. And his last birthday in June had been his twentieth.

The low wail of bagpipes and the rhythmic beating of drums penetrated William's consciousness. The British were advancing on the American positions. He strained to see the red-coated soldiers. His eyes could not penetrate the dense fog. The enemy was still a ways off, but they were coming closer all the time.

William's father had not wanted him to join the militia. After all, weren't his two older brothers serving. Jacob, the oldest, was a Captain on General Jackson's staff. Jeremiah, the next oldest, had joined the Tennessee Volunteer Militia a year ago. His regiment was off in the Alabama territory trying to prevent the British from taking the port of Mobile.

William hunkered down behind the big bale of cotton General Andrew Jackson had seized from the local docks. This cover gave him a false feeling of safety. The big pirate leaned back against the bale and closed his eyes. William realized the big man was trying to rest before the battle.

William studied the bale in front of him. The cotton had been densely packed, wrapped in a loose knit burlap, and securely tied with hemp twine. The fall cotton harvest had been brought to the docks for shipment to the mills in England, but the war had prevented the harvest from being shipped. The bales were now a major part of the earthworks protecting the American soldiers.

This defensive wall would stop a musket ball and probably some cannon shot. The "Cotton Wall," as some men called it, or the "Line Jackson," as the officer staff called it, would be good protection in the coming fight. The Army had worked for the last three weeks building these defenses on the north side of an old, dry canal named Rodriguez. Dirt had been piled up on the northern bank of the canal. The men had dug the canal deeper to make it harder for attackers to climb. The cotton bales were placed on top of the dirt to form the wall. The canal ran straight East from the Mississippi River to the Cypress Swamp on the edge of the Chalmette Plantation.

General Jackson had chosen the best ground for the battle. The American forces could not be flanked on either side. The field to the South of the canal had been used to grow cotton. Now, the field sat wide open with just the harvest debris to cover the ground. Some of the debris had been cleared to provide a better field of fire. There would be no hiding places for the enemy and no shooting cover for them.

On New Year's Day the British had bombarded the American line for three hours. Every day since that cannonade, the British had fired their cannons at the "Line Jackson" a few times. There had been some damage from the British bombardment. Three of the Americans' cannons had been knocked out, and some of the earthworks in front of the bales were torn up. The British infantry had made several probing attacks on the American line, but the line held.

William's company had been in the rear during those actions. Now, he was in the middle of the line. He had never been in a shooting fight where he would be trying to kill men, and they would be trying to kill him. In fact, he had never killed a man in anger or for any other reason. There had been a few fights back home, but those fights had been with fists or in wrestling matches. Some were serious, but no one really got hurt. In this fight, however, someone would get hurt, and some men surely would get killed.

With the bagpipes blaring louder now, the British were closing in. The fog was still very heavy. More light filled the eastern sky, and still he could see only twenty-to-thirty feet into the dense fog. If he couldn't see the enemy, he reassured himself, then they couldn't see him either. He wasn't sure if that was a good thing or a bad thing.

The British were coming. The big pirate moved his musket to a ready position, checking the load. This motion reminded William to check his rifle. James Woods, the man on the other side of William, checked his rifle, too. James was a neighbor and good friend from back home. They had grown up together. When the call for volunteers had come, they had joined the militia together.

James had dusty brown hair and brown eyes and was

about William's size and weight. Both carried the same number of years, but James was five months older than William. Their parents had come over the mountains from Virginia to Tennessee together. They had settled the same area and located their farms only a few miles apart.

William turned his attention back to the pirate. In addition to his musket, the pirate carried a thirty-inch cutlass that hung from a strap on his waist band, and a pistol and a knife were stuck in his belt. William and James were armed alike, with long rifles and hunting knives. When William left for the Army, William's father had given his favorite rifle to William. The weapon was accurate and trustworthy. Several times he had used it in shooting matches. Most of the matches William had won.

He shivered again. The cold morning air penetrated his buckskin jacket, and despite the warmth of the home-spun cotton shirt his mother had made, he felt cold. The men in the militia didn't have uniforms, just the clothes they brought from home. The manner of dress often bespoke the occupation of the wearer. Hunters and farmers wore buckskins. City fellows and storekeepers wore breeches and frock coats with top hats.

"All you men who have long rifles, get ready; the enemy is almost in range. Those with muskets hold back and wait for the order to fire muskets." The order was barked by the lieutenant of their militia company.

How did the lieutenant know the British were about in range? William thought. *He could not see a darn thing in the dim light and fog. And what good did it do to shoot into the fog at the sounds of the approaching soldiers he couldn't see. He was a pretty good shot when he could see what he was shooting, but shooting through the fog didn't make sense.*

He started to protest, but as if reading William's mind, the big pirate said softly, "De British, dey bunch up and form lines as dey come toward de enemy. All we haft to do is fire at de sounds, and we will probably hit dem and reduce d'eir number considerably."

Jock's explanation made some sense. A long rifle shot would carry much farther than the musket ball. He steadied his rifle on the cotton bale and aimed at the approaching sounds. The bagpipes were much louder, and he began to hear the soft shuffle of many feet. *But how would the lieutenant know when they were in range?*

He didn't have time to think about this. The order came.

"LONG RIFLES . . . FIRE!" The air split with gun fire. He saw James' shoulder recoil as he squeezed his shot off. William aimed where he thought the enemy might be and squeezed the trigger. The gun recoiled into his shoulder hard. It hurt and he exclaimed out loud, but no one heard him over the roar of the battle. He had been so concerned about seeing the enemy through the fog that he had forgotten one of the first lessons his father had taught him when he learned to shoot. *William, always keep the butt of the rifle tight against your shoulder so the recoil doesn't hit you and break something. Reload as fast as you can and fire another round.* he said to himself.

"LONG RIFLES KEEP FIRING," someone yelled.

Several rounds were fired by the rifles before the order "MUSKETS . . . FIRE" came, and the big pirate pulled the trigger and sent his musket ball into the fog at the sounds the British were making. The sounds of orders being shouted could be heard over the din. William fired again. The sounds of the bagpipes had dropped to one-or-two pipers, and the drummers' beat had almost stopped completely.

"RELOAD . . . FIRE AT WILL!"

The sound of gun fire was all around him. The cannons booming came over the noise of the rifle and musket fire. Gun smoke mingled with the fog and burnt his eyes. Seeing more than a few feet became impossible.

18

The British were firing back. Bullets were hitting the cotton bales in front of them. The bale, two away from James, absorbed a cannon ball, lifting and flinging the bale in the air and backwards as the ball buried itself deep inside. The sudden slamming backward of the bale sent the men behind it sprawling, but they quickly regained their footing pushing the cotton bale back in place and began firing again.

The big pirate shouted over the noise, "Glad we got des bales, huh."

James suddenly jerked and spun around; blood spurted from his wound. He fell backwards and grabbed his shoulder. The sight of James' blood filled William with an overpowering fear. An uncontrollable panic filled his mind. *RUN!* He turned to get away. They were going to kill him.

The big pirate glanced at William. Instantly, his big, powerful hand grabbed William's arm in a vise-like-grip that shut off the blood flow. He knew William was ready to run.

"RELOAD," he shouted, jerking William back behind the bale. "KEEP SHOOTING!"

The pirate's unexpected grip calmed William some, but he still wanted out of there. As if in a haze, he automatically began reloading his rifle repeating to himself: *(1) clean the bore with a wad, (2) pour powder down the muzzle, (3) ram a wad down the barrel, (4) tamp it down with the Ram Rod, (5) drop the ball . . . .*

There was movement in front of the bale. The smoke and fog were so thick he wasn't sure at first. But then he saw a red-coated soldier climbing over the bale in front of him. The soldier was using another soldier as a ladder. As the Redcoat climbed the bale, it moved, opening a space between the bales. William could see the Redcoat's bare knees beneath his kilt. The soldier's musket with its bayonet sticking way out in front sent a feeling of fear

19

through William's whole being.

The pirate's pistol fired. The Highlander fell, to be replaced by another much closer. He had pushed his way between the bales. William stepped back tripping over James. The Scotsman came with his bayonet pointed right at William's chest. James brought his rifle up with his left hand, firing too quickly, missing the soldier. Suddenly, a cutlass penetrated deep in the soldier's side. Over went the Redcoat with the cutlass caught in a bind between his ribs. As the Redcoat fell, the pirate, trying to pull the cutlass free, turned away from the protection of the bales. The fall of the soldier jerked the cutlass from the pirate's hand, causing him to turn his back to the space between the bales.

Another Redcoat appeared in the space between the bales. He thrust his bayonet toward the pirate's back. William had recovered his footing and without thinking, he pushed the barrel of his rifle up under the Redcoat's bayonet, turning it away from the pirate. Stepping forward, William brought the butt of his rifle up under the soldier's chin with all the strength he could muster. The Redcoat's head flew backward; he dropped his musket and tumbled back, down out of sight into the canal. No more of the enemy came up the body ladder towards them. William finished reloading and fired at the retreating red shadows.

"FIRE AGAIN; THEY'RE RUNNING," someone shouted.

"DON'T LET THEM GET AWAY," someone else shouted. And men started over the bales.

"HALT . . . RELOAD," came the order from the officers up and down the line.

"THEY ARE REFORMING FOR ANOTHER GO AT US!" One officer shouted.

The British tried again and again to breach the American defenses, but they never got as close as they had on the first charge. Their numbers had been thinned too much.

After that, there was no more fight left in the British. The British retreated. The "CEASE FIRE" order could be heard up and down the line, and the firing died away to be replaced by the cries and shrieks of the wounded.

As the smoke cleared and the fog burned off, the Americans could see British bodies littering the field in front of the line. The moans of the wounded seemed to be all around them. The dead Redcoats and Highlanders were piled two and three deep in some places.

This sight William would never forget, and one he hoped would never be repeated. It made him feel very sick inside. The contents of his stomach started up his throat. He turned to the back of their position so as to not be seen by the others as he threw-up. He was not alone. There were a few cheers as the British retreated, but not many.

Such a waste of good men. William was happy for the victory and sad and disturbed at the cost. True the British were the enemy and wanted to gain control of his country and its people. Without this victory he might be forced to live under British tyrannies. He knew that Americans must be ready to fight for their freedom and the right to live the way they chose. The Americans had been attacked. The President's House and Washington City had been burned. The President and the Congress had been made to retreat and hide. All along the frontier, the British had been inciting the Indians to attack American settlements. There had been no choice but to fight; however, that didn't mean anyone enjoyed the letting of so much blood. But now wasn't the time to ponder the merits of their cause. Where the redcoats had breached the line, William and the big pirate pushed the cotton bales back into place.

Together they began adding dirt to help hold the

bales in case the British attacked again. As they worked behind the bale they could not see carnage on the battlefield.

"Grab your guns, they're coming at us again!" a man nearby cried.

William stood up and looked at the battlefield. To his astonishment he saw dead soldiers getting up from the ground and from behind piles of bodies. But they were not attacking; they were leaving their weapons and coming toward the American line.

"Keep your guns on them boys," Captain Stewart, the company commander, yelled.

"Take them prisoner," a strong deep voice shouted. William looked toward the sound of the command. General Jackson stood on top of a cotton bale not very far down the line, issuing commands and directions to his officers.

Some of the regular Army troops climbed over the barricades and began herding these surrendering British soldiers behind the line into a holding area.

"Des British, dey been playing dead so dey not get killed," the pirate commented. "Der must be several hundred of dem."

Some of the British soldiers had blood on their uniforms where they had been wounded. William watched until the last of the Redcoats disappeared behind the line. He described the sight to James who had remained behind the cotton bale. He hadn't felt like moving a whole lot because of his wound.

When William turned his attention back to James, he was leaning back against a bale. Someone knelt by his side looking at the wound. It turned out the man examining James was a doctor from another militia company.

"It's not as bad as I first thought," the doctor told James. "The bullet has torn a piece of muscle just under the arm. You need some sewing young fellow, but you will live. You are going to feel puny for a few days from the loss of blood." The doctor gave James the option of being treated right there or going to the medical tent for treatment. He chose the immediate treatment where he sat. No one wanted to go to the medical tent. Very few good stories came from that place.

James allowed as how the wound hurt like the blazes.

The doctor gave James a big swig of whiskey, proceeded to clean the wound with whiskey, and then sewed and bandaged it. James ground his teeth on a piece of wood the doctor had given him while William held the arm up and steady so the doctor could see to work. James was strong. He only cried out a couple of times. William was not at all sure he could have gone through what James did without yelling his head off.

William's company had done well: two men wounded and none were killed.

Captain Stewart, the company commander, walked around checking on all his men. As he came by William, he said, "Saw what you did. Good move. You saved this man's life," pointing to the big pirate.

William said, "He saved my life when the wall was breached. All I did was react when the next soldier came through."

"You reacted well. I'll put it in my report, William," said the Captain.

He then turned to James, "You did well today. I'm glad your wound isn't too serious. You'll be back on duty in no time."

James just nodded. He didn't feel like talking. His shoulder hurt too much.

The Captain then turned to the big pirate and said, "You're a good man in a fight. I'd like to have you with us any time. What is your name?"

The pirate grinned and said, "Thank ye kindly, yer

Honor. Jock Smith at yer service, Sir," knuckling his cap as seamen do when reporting to an officer. "I might just tag along with ye boys. Ye're good fighting men."

"Well, I hope there is no more fighting for a while anyway," replied Captain Stewart. "You're welcome to join us anytime."

Jock the pirate looked at William, "Ye saved my life."

"And you saved mine," responded William.

"That makes us blood brothers and bound fer life," Jock stated.

James just looked at them as they shook hands at this pronouncement. He was hurting bad, but felt better when Jock said to him, "You fought well, shooting with one hand to save yer friend. Ye are part of our brotherhood, too." He pumped James' good arm, causing a wince.

William was glad his friend had been included.

How long had the battle been? William wondered. It seemed long, but according to the Captain, in reality, it had been only a little over an hour. Short as battles go.

They were exhausted and hungry. There had been no time to eat that morning. They had been roused from sleep and rushed to the barricades before daylight.

"The British are on their way" was all they had been told. William had some beef jerky and passed it out. His canteen was only half full of water from last night. He offered it to the others. The pirate smiled and produced, from who knows where, a bottle of red wine. It tasted great with the jerky.

William finished eating and stood up. He looked down the line. Henry Schmitt, with his surly, crooked smile, was standing about fifty feet away looking at him. William had not seen him there before the battle. It made him feel very uneasy to think Henry had been that close during the battle. Henry was always trouble for William. Every time their paths crossed, Henry tried to pick a fight.

"So you made it, you little cheater. Too bad . . . .You should have been shot instead of James," he said.

There was no love lost between them. Henry had never forgiven William for beating him in a shooting match six years earlier. He claimed William had cheated because William didn't hold his rifle in the conventional way. William's father had attached a carrying-strap to the rifle, and William wrapped the strap around his hand to steady the gun for better aiming. William had beaten Henry by hitting the most targets dead center. The prize of five silver dollars had gone to William. Henry and his father had complained bitterly to the judge, to no avail.

Henry was about William's height but carried twenty-to-thirty pounds more. He was four years older with the attitude of *I'm older, so I'm better than you*. He had dirty brown hair and an ugly stubble of beard on his chin which complemented his sullen look. His dark brown eyes sent a piercing message of hate. The clothes he wore were badly stained and grimy. There was a mean streak in him as there was in his father and brother. It showed in his face and made it unattractive.

There had been a couple of run-ins with Henry back in Tennessee when the Schmitts had come to William's home county for some shooting event. These dust-ups were words and accusations, but not pleasant. William had done his best to avoid Henry. He was in a different regiment from William's, but they were both volunteers in the Tennessee militia. William had seen him a few times on the march to New Orleans, but there had been no words exchanged. This stony silence was just as well because William wanted nothing to do with Henry.

William said nothing, and not wanting trouble, he turned his attention back to James and his pirate friend Jock. Henry muttered something more that William could not understand; he simply ignored it.

Chapter Two

After the Battle

Stories of the battle began to filter in as other members of the company joined the three men or passed by. Each seemed to have a story or two to tell of the fight. William's company had acquitted itself well. No one had run. William knew he had panicked and almost had run. He felt ashamed but said nothing.

The artillery battery on the West bank of the Mississippi River had played a big part in the British defeat. They had poured canister and grape shot into the British lines. The British had sent a force to the West bank to capture the battery, but they were late. By the time the British force captured the American battery, the battle was over and the British were in retreat. The commander of that force reluctantly returned the battery to the Americans and retreated to the British positions on the East bank.

Another pirate came by where James, William, and Jock were sitting, "Ye coming back to de swamp, Jock?" he asked the big man.

"No, I think I'll stay with des men fer a while. I like

de cut of d'eir jib," he replied.

"I tell Lafitte when I see him, Jock. He will be sorry to lose ye to Land Lubbers," the pirate said as he moved on.

Jacob came by to check on William. After meeting Jock, saying hello to James and inquiring about his wound, he asked William about the fight, and insuring himself that William was alright, he left. Duty called.

William began to study his new friend, the pirate, Jock Smith. If it weren't for the scar on his cheek, he would not be a bad looking man. His big friendly smile was engaging. He was hefty and powerful though not intimidating. There seemed to be gentleness about him now the fight was over. His movements were fluid and unencumbered. He gave the impression of being quite capable of handling himself very well in a fight or anything else he set his mind to. William guessed his age to be twenty or twenty-one. Although his three-or-four day growth of black beard made him look older, his accent said he was of British decent.

Jock wore an old blue jacket and dirty, white seaman pants. These were a sharp contrast to his highly-polished, silver-buckle shoes. A red bandana was tied around his head with his wispy, black hair protruding at the back. His blue eyes conveyed an intelligence William had not expected from a pirate.

How did Jock feel about fighting the British? William wondered. *After all he was British before he became a pirate. But, he had referred to the enemy as the British. Didn't he think of himself as being British? These questions would be for another time when they knew each other better.*

Jock told William and James how he began his sailor's life. He figured he was nine-or-ten then, but he didn't know for sure. After his father had died from unknown causes, he had gone to sea as a Cabin Boy on a merchantman, the *Weavertree,* out of London. It was a sleek, two-masted ship. His father had been a carpenter who worked at whatever jobs he could get to support his wife and son. He taught Jock how to use the tools of his trade and how to recognize good wood when he found it.

After three years aboard the *Weavertree,* Jock had managed to move from Cabin Boy to Apprentice to the ship's Carpenter. Wooden boats always needed repairing, and he knew how to work with wood. His father had taught him well. Jock learned how to repair the ship's many parts and to create new ones when needed.

Jock told of his capture by the pirates. His ship had been sailing off the coast of Barbados on the way to New England with a cargo of rum. The *Weavertree* had been attacked. The Captain tried to outrun the pirate ship, but the *Weavertree* had been too slow. The *Weavertree's* crew had put up a good fight, firing their cannons at the pirates to slow them down. But the pirate ship had twenty, 16-pounders on its deck. The *Weavertree* only had six, 12-pounders and two, deck swivel guns. The swivel guns were to repel boarders. They had not been used. Being badly out-gunned and overwhelmed by the pirate's faster ship and superior forces, the *Weavertree* eventually had to surrender.

The pirates needed a carpenter because theirs had been killed in a previous engagement. As soon as they found out Jock was a carpenter, he was impressed into the pirate crew. The pirate ship turned out to be one of Jean Lafitte's fleet with a captain named Brown--a mean one from Jock's description of him. Lafitte had spotted Jock when Captain Brown's ship returned to Barataria, Lafitte's headquarters in the Mississippi Delta. Once at Barataria, the pirate plunder was unloaded and then sent to Lafitte's warehouse in New Orleans to be sold.

When Jock proved to be a good ship's carpenter, Lafitte bargained him away from Captain Brown and made him the ship's carpenter aboard Lafitte's ship, *La Diligent*. Jock had been a pirate ever sii pirates claimed no nationality or country. They were members of the pirate brotherhood.

"Alright, enough of this lollygagging. We want to get those dead British out from in front of us. Some of you able bodied men get a few of those stretchers and help carry those Redcoats over to the British lines. Leave your guns here," a major ordered.

The British medical and burial details were at work in the field. They seemed grateful for the help but said nothing to the Americans. Many of the wounded had already been taken to the British lines. It was a grizzly business, and William was glad when he could return to the American lines. Meantime, other men had been repairing the Cotton Wall as best they could, just in case of another attack.

The Americans stayed on the line, ready if the British renewed their attack. Lookouts kept a watch on the British lines in case they began forming to fight some more. Fortunately, no new attack came. All fight seemed to have gone out of the British.

During the following two weeks the Americans repaired their defenses and remained vigilant. The British buried their dead, treated their wounded, and rested. A rumor spread through the American forces that the British commanding general and three top commanders had been killed during the battle. William got a chance to ask Jacob about the rumor, and he confirmed that American intelligence had learned the British Commander General Pakenham had been killed, as well as, several high ranking officers. Jacob also told William that the British ranks had been decimated by the American cannon and rifle fire. His estimate of the British losses would be over 2,000 killed, wounded, missing, or captured. These British losses were overwhelming when compared to the

American losses of less than 100.

Two weeks after the battle, the British got back on their ships and sailed away leaving no residual force to hold their position.

Over a month after the battle, the American camp erupted in cheers. The war had ended. A treaty known as the Treaty of Ghent--ending the war--had been signed several weeks before the battle. Neither side had known. Thus, the Battle of New Orleans had been fought after the war had ended. The news of the treaty had arrived too late.

General Andrew Jackson had become a national hero. Every newspaper in the country had heaped accolades on him for his defeat of the superior British forces. The American morale ran very high. As soon as Jackson became convinced the war had ended he began to disband the fine group of Army men he had assembled.

The New Orleans's free black brigade, made up of free black men, was quickly dismissed so they could return to their homes. The Indian Companies of Choctaw and Shawnee Warriors were also started back to their homes in Alabama, Mississippi, and Tennessee.

The Tennessee Volunteer Regiments, mostly made up of men who had signed up for six months, would be the next to start home. Their short term enlistments would expire in March, April, and May. Soon these units needed to start the long hike to Nashville or Knoxville, depending upon where the men had enlisted. William's and James' militia company consisted of men who had enlisted in Nashville in November. Their enlistments would expire in April. The walk back to Nashville would take about five to six weeks. That meant they must start for home before the end of March.

Jock had said he liked having solid ground under his feet instead of a rolling deck. He did not wish to return to being a pirate. All of the pirates who fought with the

Americans had been offered pardons for their service against the British. Jock accepted the pardon.

William and James liked their new friend, Jock, and asked him to come to Tennessee with them. William assured Jock that his carpentry skills would provide plenty of work opportunities. James agreed with William. The three men were developing a strong friendship that could last a life time. Captain Stewart liked having Jock as part of the militia company. So Jock agreed to walk with the company to Tennessee.

Chapter Three

Peace

The Second War of Independence had ended with the crushing defeat of the British at New Orleans. The British hopes of decolonizing America and taking control of the Northwest Territories had been destroyed at the battle for New Orleans city. Therefore, the Louisiana Territory remained firmly in the hands of the Americans.

General Jackson began the business of returning the city of New Orleans back to its civilian authorities. To improve the city's defenses, he ordered a fort to be built on the west bank of the Mississippi where the artillery batteries had been. This fort would guard the water approach to the city. The work would keep the Army occupied while it was slowly disbanded. Keeping soldiers busy was more important than providing the protection specified.

Those Regiments to be discharged, including men with enlistments due to expire in March, left immediately for their places of origin. Each militia company was ordered to improve the roads and the bridges on their march home.

The remaining Army units were put to work repairing levies and roads. In some cases, roads were extended farther away from the city to accommodate commerce. New roads were being built north toward the northern villages and settlements.

William's company, whose enlistments would not expire until April, remained in camp outside of New Orleans to work on the fort. The men, however, were ready to start the 700-mile walk to Nashville. Captain Stewart disappointed them with the news that the fort must be finished before they could leave. That meant it would be the middle of March before the long hike started.

Jock and William worked hard at the tasks assigned to them and looked forward to getting leave to go into New Orleans. Because of James' wound, the officers limited his duties to light work. The officers found plenty of jobs to keep all the men busy. The promised time off in New Orleans city finally came. Jock had visited the city a number of times during his pirate days. He told his new friends about some sporting places that he wanted to show them.

The Paymaster had arrived with a portion of their pay, so the men had money in their pockets. Plus, William had the ten silver dollars his father had given him when he left for the Army. These coins were kept separate in a small leather bag. James' father had also given him some money when he left home. Jock had some money from his pirate days, so they were well fixed to buy a good meal and a bottle of wine and maybe to see a dancing girl show. The meal was the most important. Army food wasn't the greatest.

The next morning, they washed up in the stream that flowed by the camp. William put on his best shirt. James did the same. Jock wore a frock coat, white shirt, black britches, and his always-present, silver-buckle shoes. He looked pretty fancy and his friends told him so.

In New Orleans the first order of business would be to find Jock some more appropriate clothes for the march to Tennessee. Buckskins would be best, if they could be found, Lindsey-Woolsey otherwise. They found a tailor shop a block off Royal Street that sold clothes people had left in payment for their new clothes. The tailor had three Buckskin Jackets in stock, one that could be made to fit Jock's large shoulders. The tailor said he could do the work and have the jacket ready in the afternoon. Pants would be another problem. None of the Buckskins were big enough. The tailor said he had some good soft leather that he could turn into a pair of pants to fit Jock. Again these would also be ready in the afternoon. A shirt for under the jacket proved easier. There were several appropriate shirts that fit Jock nicely.

William bought a new shirt to replace the one his mother had made for him when he left for the Army. The old shirt had holes in the elbows and the seams were splitting. All the heavy work he had been doing caused his shoulders and arms to muscle up quite a bit. The old shirt no longer fit very well.

James didn't buy anything saying he was fine for now. The friends left the shop happy with their purchases. The next door cobbler shop supplied Jock with some moccasins and some walking boots. Finally, it was time to start looking for a good meal.

As they turned the corner onto Bourbon Street, William ran right into Henry Schmitt and four of his Army friends.

"Watch where you're going," Henry slurred, drink affecting his speech. "Oh it's you, you little shooting cheat . . . get out-a-my-way." He was drunk and smelled of cheap whiskey. Henry steadied himself with a hand on one of his none-too-steady friends. They obviously had been drinking for some time, maybe all night because it wasn't even noon.

"Hello, Henry," William said. "Sorry I didn't see you," apologizing, not wanting to start trouble seeing that Henry was being very unfriendly. Making a path for Henry, William stepped to one side.

"Well, watch where you're going. Get out of my way!" As Henry said that, he put his hand on Williams' chest and shoved him backwards. Henry obviously was looking for a fight.

"Don't do that," William said.

Henry Schmitt had a weight and age advantage over William. Henry moved his hand ready to shove William again. His hand came toward William's chest with his fingers pointed up. He was planning to catch William squarely with the heel of his hand and deliver a blow to knock William down. When the hand came forward, William grabbed it in both hands. His thumbs pressed hard against Henry's palm, bending Henry's wrist back toward his arm. With a surprised cry, Henry dropped to his knees.

William's move had been so quick and unexpected that Henry was down in a wrist lock before he knew what had happened. Henry shouted in pain as William pushed hard on Henry's palm extracting another yell.

One of the other men started toward the struggling men.

"Let dem be," Jock said.

The man took in Jock's size and obvious strength, thought better of his action and stepped back.

William could see Henry's other hand was behind him reaching for something.

"You pull that knife, Henry, and I'll break your wrist and maybe your arm," he warned. "Now, we don't want any trouble. You're drunk, so we'll make allowances for your bad behavior. You boys," taking in the other four, "go on back to your camp and sleep it off."

William's voice reflected strength and authority.

Henry's friends were none too happy about this. They had the advantage of numbers, and James had one arm in a sling. Henry was cussing and making all kinds of threats against William and his family, but he couldn't move because of the hold William had on him.

Just then, two men came up beside James. James turned to them and said "Hello, Sam, Mathew. How are you fellows doing today?"

"Not bad," Sam replied. "It looks like you've got a varmint by the tail there, William. What you goanna do with him?"

"Well, I don't know." Turning toward the four men that stood behind Henry, William said, "I'll turn Henry loose if you will take him back to camp and put him to bed. We're not wanting a fight, but if you push us, we will oblige. Well, . . . what will it be?" he demanded.

Henry's friends were looking at the four men beside William not liking the odds. They had sobered up quite a bit in the last few minutes. One said, "Come on, Henry. let's go on back to camp. We need some sleep. We start for Knoxville tomorrow." He took Henry under his free arm, and another man stepped forward gripping Henry under the arm William was holding. William released Henry's hand.

Henry shook his hand to get the blood flowing again. As he was hauled away, he sent out a scream of curses toward William and his friends.

William turned to Sam and Mathew, "Thanks for your help. We are on our way to a restaurant to have a good meal. Will you join us?"

"You bet," Sam replied. "We're looking for some food and a drink or two, too."

"Jock knows a place down the street that he thinks is good."

"What are we waiting for? Let's go!"

Jock fell in beside William and said softly, "Dat man hates ye. He'll kill ye if he gets a chance."

William hadn't thought *it was that serious. The trouble between Henry and him had just been Henry trying to pick a fight, nothing more, until now. Then, he discounted it because Henry had been drunk.*

"Henry Schmitt lives with his father and brother North of the Holston River. That's a long way from our farm. I doubt if I will ever see him again. We heard them say their company was starting back tomorrow. We won't leave for at least another couple of weeks or more."

"None-de-less, watch out for him," Jock said. "Ye just humiliated him in front of his friends. He will want revenge. He's a killer."

William said nothing, but Jock's strong words remained in his mind.

Chapter Four

The Mysterious Dancer

Bourbon Street was lined on both sides with cantinas, restaurants, and shops of every sort. Signs were hung over many of the doorways advertising their specialties. A sign with a woman in a fancy blue dress told of a dress shop, another with a Beaver Top Hat identified a men's shop, and on another simply the word Carlo's identified a restaurant.

All sorts of people filled the street. A well-appointed barouche with a uniformed driver sat parked in front of the Blue Dress Shoppe. Several horses were tied to hitching posts or statues of small boys holding rings in outstretched hands. The pungent odor of horses mixed with the aromas of food cooking assaulted their noses. It was offensive and exhilarating at the same time.

Jock led them toward a large sign that read *The Pirates Cove and Refuge.*

"Dis place is owned by a former pirate cook who became tired of de pirate life after being wounded. With his prize money, he opened dis restaurant. Using an iron fist of discipline, he makes sure dat his restaurant does not become a bawdy, drinking, rough house. He provides a clean, safe place to enjoy good food and quiet conversation. His reputation as an excellent chef and purveyor of fine wines has earned him the patronage of local businessmen and society. De restaurant's name gives patrons de thrill of danger and being around dangerous people while being perfectly safe," Jock explained.

When the five men entered, they were greeted with wonderful aromas of beef cooking over an open fire. The owner, a corpulent man named Pirate Slim, greeted Jock like a long lost cousin. He warmly welcomed each of the men. They were taken to a round table with a white cotton table cloth away from the kitchen door.

Soon they were enjoying boiled shrimp with a spicy, tomato dipping-sauce and fresh baked bread with butter. Next, the waiter brought Roast Beef with potatoes, carrots, and onions covered in a rich gravy. A bottle of French, red wine came with the meal. For dessert they had a very cold custard covered with fresh strawberries. Everyone agreed it was an excellent meal.

The conversation flowed easily. They talked of home and families and what each planned to do when they got back there. Sam and Mathew lived on farms north of Russellville, the village of William and James. Sam had been married for several years and had two children, a boy six and a girl three. He had only enlisted for six months because he wanted to be home for spring planting. He hated being away from his family but felt duty-bound to serve at least one hitch in the militia. His brother who lived on the next farm had been willing to look after his family while he served his hitch.

Mathew's farm was small, just large enough to raise a few hogs and a milk cow. Most of the time he earned his living by driving freight wagons for William's uncle. Mathew's wife had a large garden that produced plenty of vegetables for his family and even enough to sell to others nearby. His wife had a green thumb. Anything would grow for her, so he said. They had no children, so far.

Mathew had enlisted for six months, also. He and Sam had journeyed to Nashville together to volunteer.

When their plates were cleaned and cleared away, the men paid the bill and wandered out onto the street. Slowly, they continued their tour of Bourbon Street, taking their time and letting their meal digest. They were feeling good and not in a hurry to return to camp. They passed a tavern from which the exciting, yet, soothing sounds of a Spanish guitar emanated.

"Come on, let's go in here and have a drink," James said, and the five men trouped into the dimly lit interior. The guitar player was sitting on a stool to one side of the door. A few tables were on one side of the room with an open area between them and the bar. Most of the tables were empty. Talking softly and sharing a bottle of wine, two men sat at the table nearest the guitar player. An older man sat alone at the table on the opposite side of the room with a mug in front of him. Three men in frocked coats sat in the back playing cards.

James selected a table in the center of the room beside the open area. A woman came from behind the bar to take their drink orders. Two bottles of red wine were ordered. She brought the wine with glasses and asked if food would be needed.

"No, thank ye kindly," said Jock, "just de wine."

They had been at the bar about a half hour when a woman stepped into the front doorway and stood surveying the room. Her face was hard to see against the bright, sun-lit background of the outside. Her long, black hair hung below her shoulders and was shiny where the sun reflected from it. She wore Spanish peasant clothes. Her white blouse was pulled off her shoulders, and her pleated skirt in a dark, brown, nondescript pattern swayed as she moved. Black slippers with little heels covered her feet.

Evaluating each person, she took her time looking around the room. Her eyes locked on William's. She stepped into the room and smiled at William. Everyone could see she was young and beautiful. All eyes were upon her. She walked over to the bartender, swinging her hips seductively with every step. She said something to him and put a coin in his hand. She then walked to the guitar player with the same suggestive gait. She said something to him and put a coin in his hand. He began to strum the guitar, producing a Spanish tune that had a rhythmic beat.

She stepped to the center of the open area, and from nowhere she produced a pair of wooden castanets. Over her thumbs, she deftly slipped the leather thongs that held the two shell-shaped pieces together. The shells rested in the palms of her hands. Slowly, she began clicking the castanets with her fingers to the beat of the guitar. She swayed one way then another gently moving to the beat. Smoothly, she floated around the room lightly tapping her heels to the strumming. Melodic and captivating, the clicking castanets drew subtle attention to the dancer who was superb. The cadence of the music grew as the dance progressed. The dancer's steps became more intricate and lively.

Everyone watched spellbound. William, who was sitting right at the edge of the dance floor, could not take his eyes from her. She, in turn, was paying attention to him. She moved close to him and gently ran her hand over his shoulder. She continued her dance, flirting with each man, but always coming back to William and always seductively placing her hand or hands on his shoulders and hair.

Jock leaned over to William and whispered, "She likes ye."

William, embarrassed and unsure what to do, realized something was happening to him. He had never seen anything like this before, and his reaction was making him uncomfortable yet also quite excited. His older brothers had talked about women they had met and the intrigues that had ensued, so he wasn't completely naïve. But he had no firsthand knowledge of a woman and what occurred between men and women. He had heard other men talk about their encounters with women in sporting places. He had not thought this was such a place.

The dance increased in energy. The dancer spun around and around. Her skirt whirled high revealing her long, bare legs and what appeared to be a white under garment.

More and more, William became her main interest. She was singling him out, as the dance rhythm intensified. He became more uncomfortable and acutely aware of his body's reaction to her attention. As the dance reached its climax, she finished right in front of him with a low curtsey, while holding her skirt out to the side with one hand. The room erupted in applause. She was breathing hard as she stood up. Her black eyes again locked on his blue ones.

She broke away, picked up a hat from William's table, and danced around to each patron holding the hat out for tips. Enough small coins were tossed into the hat that it jingled by the time she returned to William. He tossed a silver dollar into the hat. She removed the coins and replaced the hat on the table. Then she took his hand and breathed with a soft Spanish accent, "Come . . . we talk."

She led him to the farthest table from the door. William pulled out the chair for her. He sat down opposite her. She looked back at Jock and said, "I come back and talk to you later." As she did this, William heard someone say, "Well, he's going to be occupied for quite a while."

She held William's hand across the table asking, "You like my dancing? Si?"

Her hand was soft and her perfume filled his senses with a beautiful aroma. The fragrance, delicately reminiscent of roses, enveloped him.

"Yes," he muttered. He was intoxicated. She was gorgeous. "My name is . . ."

She touched her fingers to his lips as he started to say his name. "No names, please . . . You may call me La Ballerina Hispañia, and I will call you Mi Amigo Americano."

"I love to dance. I want to be a professional dancer and perform all over Europe and America."

"Then," she continued, "I want to go to Spain to study. I have relatives there who will help me become a great dancer. Here, I dance for tips to earn enough money to pay for my passage and my training when I get there."

Caught up in her enthusiasm, he gushed, "You're already a great dancer."

"Ah, how many dancers have you seen?"

"Uh, you're the first Spanish Dancer I've ever seen. But I've seen Irish jig dancers back home who were very good."

"Ah, but the Irish only have a few steps," she scoffed, "while the Spanish have many."

As the afternoon progressed, they talked of her dancing and her mother's training. He told her of his family's farm and his plan to raise thoroughbred horses and of his desire to own a farm and have a family and children. She asked questions about his family and friends and the battle against the British. He did not want their time together to end.

"I want to see you again. I can get leave to come into the city in two days. Will you meet me?" he asked, fearing she might leave, and he would never see her again.

There was a long pause before she answered.

"There is a small park two blocks from here. I sometimes go there to read in the afternoon."

Rising slowly, she said, "I have to go to the little house."

Was she exhibiting the hard edge to her personality he had noticed several times during their conversation? It seemed out of place with her softer personality traits. It didn't fit with the descriptions of her parents.

"I be right back and we talk some more," she said, as she went out the door at the back of the room. He had not seen that door before. As she opened the door, a small court yard, bathed in sun light, appeared. She waved and closed the door.

He sat back in the chair thinking about this wonderful experience and waiting for her return. After ten minutes when she did not return, he got up and opened the door to the yard.

Across the yard was a privy. The door had been left open, and he could see the empty bench. Lying on the ground in front of the privy was a small piece of paper. William crossed the grass to the paper and picked it up. It read:

Mi Amigo Americano,
I am sorry. I could not return. I will see you in two days.
La Ballerina Hispañia

She had gone. The door leading from the court yard to the alley stood partially open. He stepped into the alley. It was empty also.

Using the privy to relieve himself, he wondered, *Will she really meet me in the park? He didn't want to face his friends, but he had no other choice.*

He opened the door to the Tavern and entered. Everyone turned expectantly looking behind him.

"She's gone," he sighed. "I guess there won't be another dance." This comment brought some chuckles.

"Oh darn, I was really looking forward to dat dance," Jock said.

Then seeing William's face and realizing he had touched a nerve, Jock added, "She probably wore herself out, anyway." He poured William a glass of wine and said, "I'm sorry, William. She really got to you, didn't she?"

William had many different feelings all mixed up in his head. *Very strong feelings. He wanted to be with her, to know her better. He wanted her to like him. What was her name? Where did she go? Why did she have to leave so quickly? He wanted to find her.* William got up and went over to the bartender.

"What is the dancer's name?" he asked.

"We call her 'The Little Spanish Dancer,'" the bartender answered.

"Does she come in here often?" William asked.

The bartender replied, "She comes in here every month or so. It's always the same. She pays for the privilege to dance for the patrons. She pays the guitar player. She dances; then sometimes she selects one young man to talk with; sometimes she simply collects her tips then goes out the back door and disappears. I never see her again until she appears in the front door. She won't be back for a month. I never know when. I never have seen her around either, so she must live outside of the city somewhere. I don't know where."

William was understandably unhappy. He wanted to find her. "I'm going to walk around some," he told the other men and went out into the late afternoon sunshine.

As his eyes adjusted to the bright light, he looked up and down the street. People were moving about or just standing and talking. There were several carriages that rolled by. A large black one caught his eye because of its odd box-like shape. It looked out of place.

The street was fairly busy. He started walking,

noticing that his shadow was growing longer. The afternoon was almost gone. Jock and James caught up with him.

"We better think about picking up your purchases and heading back to camp. It will be dark soon," James said, as he came alongside of William.

William's friends seemed to understand his mood and didn't say much. They picked up their purchases.

"She told me of a small park two blocks from the tavern that she sometimes visits in the afternoon. In two days, when I get leave again, I will be there waiting."

"Well, we must get back to camp tonight, but hopefully she will meet ye," Jock said, as they walked toward camp in the gathering gloom.

Chapter Five

Secret Meeting

Excitement grew in William as he walked into New Orleans. He was on his way to meet a beautiful girl that he really liked. She had said she would meet him in the small park by the river where she goes to read. The small doubts that had flickered through his mind the last two days crept into his thoughts again: *Would she be there? Would she feel the same as he? Why was she so mysterious about her name and family?* He suppressed these doubts preferring to think positively.

The park was right where Jock had told him it would be. There were several walking paths and benches with large oak and elm trees strategically located to provide shade for the benches. After all, the New Orleans sun could be very intense when it was out, and today there wasn't a cloud in the sky. The grass had been cut low and the paths were well-trimmed. Someone took good care of this park.

His anticipation and anxiety had pushed him to be early, but his eagerness to see the Spanish Dancer again had made him almost run to the park. How long would he have to wait? He didn't know. She had only said "afternoon." He had heard a church bell sound the call for noon mass when he entered the city. Selecting a bench near the street, he sat and pulled from his pocket the small copy of the New Testament his mother had given him. Trying to concentrate on reading while keeping an eye on the carriages and the people passing by, proved to be difficult for William.

An hour passed very slowly. The small doubts were beginning to play tricks in his mind again. *Did he have the right park? He knew of no other. Maybe she could not come today. Maybe she wouldn't be here because she didn't want to see him again.* Taking charge and concentrating on the chapter of John that he was trying to read, he forced these thoughts from his mind.

A passing carriage caught his attention because it was not like most of the landaus. *Was it that strange box-like carriage he remembered seeing two days before? He wasn't sure, but how many ugly carriages could there be?* It was stained black with an enclosed passenger compartment. Most carriages had folding canvas tops. There were open windows in the doors and a small glass-covered window beside the passenger seat. The passenger seat sat well back from the door so that the passengers could see out without being seen.

The horses were a beautifully matched pair of sorrels with white-blazed foreheads and each had four white stockings. The driver wore a top hat pulled down over his forehead and a dark green cape trimmed with a thin strip of tan cloth. His collar had been turned up in a manner that obscured most of his face. This was curious because the air had a warm, comfortable feel. The carriage appeared to be empty. William watched the carriage pass the park for the second time.

The carriage then turned down the road that ran along on the south side of the park and stopped. The driver got down and started checking the harnesses and patting the horses to reassure them of his presence. Then, he climbed back to the driver's seat and tried to find a comfortable position. *He must have been waiting for someone or just resting before picking up the carriage owner*, William thought. *He assumed the carriage was privately owned and not for hire.* He wondered, *why he made this assumption because why would someone want to own such an unattractive carriage.* The driver had paid no attention to anyone in the park. William returned to reading the passage from John.

Someone sat down next to him. It was the dancer wearing a delightfully, mischievous smile. She had come up behind him while he sat looking at that big carriage.

"I got here without your seeing me or hearing me," she exclaimed laughing, "and you a hunter and woodsman," she teased.

"You were very quiet," William said smiling. Her beautiful face was framed by her long, black hair that covered her bare shoulders. The dark eyes that looked on him twinkled with merriment at her joke. Her clothes were the same ones she had worn when she danced.

"I have been watching that big black carriage over there and wondering about its owner," he remarked.

"Is it not ugly? I would not own a carriage like that, but the horses are beautiful. I love beautiful horses," she replied.

"It's good to see you again. I was afraid that maybe I was in the wrong park, or, worst of all, that you might not come."

"Oh no, I told you I would be here and here I am, so you need not worry," she replied with just a hint of a Spanish accent.

The afternoon passed quickly as they chatted and walked around the park--sometimes holding hands, sometimes just sitting and looking at each other. He told her more about his home and family, about his dreams for the future. She talked of her plans to study dancing and music and to become an entertainer. She barely mentioned her family.

The shadows were getting long when she told him she had to leave.

"You must promise *not* to watch me leave," she said.

"Only if you promise to meet me again," he replied.

"I promise, but in the tavern tomorrow afternoon, I will dance for you again. Now, turn away and count to 100."

He turned saying, "until tomorrow then." He faced south. As he counted, he noticed the black carriage had gone. He had been so engaged with her that he had not seen it leave. He would have liked to have seen who got into the carriage.

At 100 he looked around, but she had disappeared. Knowing he would see her the next day, he went back to camp happy.

Jock and James listened as William told of his afternoon with the dancer and his planned meeting the next day. They asked if they could join him at the tavern, and he agreed. It would be good for her to meet his friends because he had told her much about them. The next day being Saturday and with no work planned for the company made getting time off easy.

The men arrived at the tavern in time to eat a lunch of some kind of a fish stew with bread. About an hour-and-a-half after they got there, she entered the tavern. She surveyed the room. Her eyes fell on William then Jock then James, and she smiled at them. Then, just as before, she paid the bartender and the guitar player and took the center of the room.

As the rhythmic melody started, she began a slow, whirling dance, clicking her castanets to the beat. Her costume today consisted of a long, black dress with a full skirt that swirled about her legs as she moved around the floor. Her pulled-back hair was held in place with a big, blue and white, flowered comb. She was absolutely gorgeous to look at and to watch. The melody slowly built, increasing in tempo, as did her movements. When the dance ended, there was applause all around. She gathered her tips then out of breath came and sat next to William. Jock and James were introduced without last names. They complimented her profusely on her dance, as did he.

As they talked of her performance, she glanced around the room. Suddenly, she stiffened, her smile disappeared, and there was fear on her face.

"I must go," she whispered.

William turned to look where she was looking. He saw a man in the shadows at a back table. He could not make out the man's features. When he turned back, she had already reached the back door. He caught up with her in the back courtyard.

"What's wrong?" he demanded, as he caught her arm to delay her flight.

"I should not have come. It is much too soon. Please let me go. I must leave quickly. You go back to your friends," she stammered, very upset.

"Not until you agree to meet me again."

"No. I cannot."

"You must agree to meet me, or I will not let you leave."

"Very well, Tuesday in the park. Now, I must go. Please do not follow." With that she pulled away from him and went out the courtyard gate into the alley.

William returned to the tavern and looked to the back table. The man had gone. As William rushed out to the street, he looked both directions. Some 50-to-60 feet north, a slightly built man was walking very rapidly away from the tavern. The man looked back, saw William, then started to run. Was he the man from the table? William couldn't be sure. James and Jock joined him, and they all started after the running man. William had always been fast and quickly began closing the distance between them, when the man turned down a side street. When William turned onto the street, it was empty. He slowed to a walk as Jock and James caught up with him. The man had vanished. They searched the street for some escape route the man could have used and found none.

The three friends returned to the tavern. They inquired with the bartender and the guitar player about the man at the back table. Neither had seen him or knew him. Right after William followed the dancer out the back door, Jock had seen the man leave. Jock described him as about five feet six inches tall, slightly built, with black, greasy hair, a large, beak-like nose and a thin, black mustache. His face was narrow and his eyes were sunk deep in his head. He had the appearance of a Spanish vaquero with a short, brown, leather jacket and leather pants that billowed out below the knee. He wore brown, leather boots with high heels.

Again William asked the bartender if he knew the name of the dancer. The bartender did not know her name. But the guitar player thought her name might be Maria. He wasn't fully sure of that. Once he had seen her talking to a big, black man on the street, and he thought the man had called her Miss Maria. Inquiries were made of the other patrons of the tavern. They did not know the dancer or the man at the back table.

That night William told Jock and James of his next meeting with the dancer.

It took forever for Tuesday afternoon to arrive, or so it seemed. But finally, here he sat waiting in the park for her to arrive. Again, he tried to read while waiting, when the black-box carriage slowly passed and turned down the street disappearing from his view. The driver had been dressed as before with his collar turned up obscuring his face. William thought no more about the carriage and returned to his book.

A small, weathered, old, black woman came toward him as he sat there. He averted his eyes. *This woman is going to ask me for money*, he thought.

She stopped directly in front of him and held out a sealed envelope saying, in a soft voice, "La Ballerina Hispañia sends this to you. She wants you go away, very dangerous, you get hurt, forget her, leave city. You leave us alone. She sent you this note. It very bad for her if you try to see her again."

He was stunned. He couldn't believe what he had just heard. He looked down at the letter. It was addressed Mi Amigo Americano. William tried to comprehend the message.

"Where is the La Ballerina Hispañia?" he demanded.

"She sent you letter to explain. You read, then go away."

William broke the seal and removed the folded paper. Carefully, he unfolded it and began to read:

Mi Amigo,

Please forgive me, I cannot meet you ever again.
Circumstances beyond my control have intervened.
Return to your home in Tennessee. I will pray for you to have a good life. Please pray for me.
With affection,
La Ballerina Hispañia

William looked up from the letter just in time to see the old, black woman turn the street corner. He ran after her, but when he turned the corner, she was nowhere to be seen. However, the big, black carriage that *Maria* had thought was so ugly, was parked a few feet down the street. William ran to the carriage and jumped on the footstep causing it to tilt. He looked inside. It was empty.

"Eye--ee!" the startled driver exclaimed. "What you

want, young master," he asked from his perch on the driver's seat.

"Did you see an old, black woman go by?" William asked.

"No. I see nothing. I sleep," answered the driver.

William looked up and down the street, but the old woman had gone. Now what was he going to do. He returned to the park and sat down on the bench trying to decide. He reread the letter.

He felt a great pain in his chest, and his mind whirled: *This beautiful girl did not want to see him ever again. Why? What was the danger? What were the uncontrolled circumstances? Was she in some kind of trouble? The old woman had said it would be bad for her if he saw her again. Why? He wanted to help and would if he could find her, but he had no clues other than that her name might be Maria and that she lived in or near the city. How does one find someone who does not want to be found? She had said she sometimes comes to the park to read. Maybe someone here knows her.*

There were several people in the park. William asked each of them if they knew or had seen her. None did. He walked up and down all of the streets surrounding the park asking about Maria but with no luck.

The walk back to camp was lonely. His company would be starting the long walk back to Tennessee in a few days. What was he going to do? He felt depressed. At Camp, he showed the letter to Jock and James. They suggested returning to the city the next day and searching for her. He agreed.

The next day the Captain allowed William to return to the city to look for this girl who had so captivated him. However, the Captain couldn't spare Jock or James, so William would have to go alone. He reminded William that they would be starting home soon.

William went to the tavern. The bartender knew no

more than yesterday. Then, William proceeded to check the taverns on the street and some that were on side streets. He found two places that knew the girl known as the Spanish Dancer. They did not know her name, not even as Maria. The scenario was always the same. She would come into the tavern. Pay to be allowed to dance. Pay the musician. Perform her dance. Then, she would disappear not to be seen again for a month or so.

William felt despondent. He returned to the small park and sat down to think. *Should he keep trying to find her? The old woman had said he put Maria in danger. What danger did he cause by continuing to look for her and would he cause her harm if he did find her?* Finally, he returned to camp and told his friends of his futile effort.

The next couple of days were very busy getting ready to start home. He couldn't get into the city until late the second afternoon. Again, he had no luck finding any clue. Even the old, black woman could not be found. *Was the dancer gone from him forever? He had to leave with the company tomorrow. Finally, he understood; he would just have to push her from his thoughts and return home. She had told him to forget her. Now, he must try to forget her. Forgetting something might be easy; forgetting someone as precious to him as was Maria, could prove to be very sad and extremely difficult.*

Chapter Six

The Sighting

Early in the morning William's regiment marched through the city as they began the long trek home. People were standing along the street and on balconies waving and cheering. The women of the sporting houses shouted the loudest. Before the militia marched into a less affluent neighborhood, the last two-story house on the street had flowers and a fountain in front and a typical, black iron balcony across the second floor.

Watching the militia march out of town, two well-dressed men stood at the near end of the balcony. At the other end of the balcony stood a well-dressed young woman. William glanced at the woman. There was something familiar. Their eyes met. He jumped. It was Maria. He shouted her name and turned to Jock who was beside him.

"There she is," he yelled, pointing at the balcony. He looked up again. An older woman stood looking at him with an angry frown. *Where'd Maria go?* He wondered.

Jock said he didn't see her. James and some of the

other men said they had only seen the older woman. Could he have mistaken the older woman for Maria? William looked at the other end of the balcony; the two men were watching him intently and not smiling.

He tried to break ranks to go knock on the door of the house. Jock stopped him. "If dat was Maria, she doesn't want to see ye. If she had wanted ye to see her, she would have waved and stayed on de balcony. Think about her message to ye. It said it would be very bad fer her ever to see ye again. Ye know des Spanish families are very protective of d'eir women folk. Ye might create a lot of trouble fer her if ye try to see her. Besides, dose two men looked very unfriendly."

Jock's logic was sound, and it stopped William from charging to her front door.

"I know it hurts to be rejected for any reason. Maybe, she's married to one of dose men, and he doesn't know she dances in taverns. Dat could explain her actions," Jock reasoned.

"Then why did she meet me twice? Why did she let me think she liked me? I don't understand," replied William, pain showing in his voice.

"I don't know," Jock said, "but it is clear dat she wants ye to forget her and stay out of her life."

William looked down at his feet. A deep sadness filled his heart. *He knew Jock was right. The Spanish Dancer had just rejected him again by disappearing when he saw her. It hurt to be unwanted by the woman he wanted to be with. This was her third rejection. He had been told "NO," and he had to accept this. He didn't understand. Why didn't she want him as much as he wanted her?* He and Jock walked on not talking.

At a fork in the road, Captain Stewart turned the company north on the river road toward Baton Rouge. The remainder of the regiment went east away from the river. William could not get Maria out of his mind. *He had seen her three times. Brief for building a relationship, but the length of time didn't matter. People fall in love at first sight. His mother had told him that. He knew he was in love with Maria. He just had to talk to her one more time. She should be the one to tell him to his face to go away. Whatever danger or trouble she had, he wanted to face it with her. He was not afraid, but, apparently, she was.*

He walked on thinking of Maria. *She had to tell him that there was no chance for them to marry and raise a family. Yes, she had talked about dancing and how she wanted to go to Spain to study and to become an entertainer. But that had to be just a young girl's fantasy, wasn't it? A dream, not really expected to happen. After all, she had told him that when her dancing career was over, she would like to marry and have a family as her mother had done. Dancers, she had explained, only have ten-to-fifteen years to dance professionally before their bodies begin to give out, and they can no longer dance and entertain. How old was she now? Sixteen, maybe seventeen. She could dance and then have children.* He walked on.

The sun climbed toward its pinnacle as the company marched north. Once in a while, glimpses of the Mississippi River could be caught through the trees that lined the road. William remained silent, deep in thought.

He was startled out of his melancholy meditation by the sharp shrill blast of a high-pitched whistle. It had an unearthly sound that he had never heard before. To a man, every one stopped walking and looked around for the source of the noise. Another screech pierced their ears. It seemed to come from the river.

"Look over there," one of the men shouted and pointed over the tree tops at the billows of grey-black smoke rising into the still blue sky. The billowing smoke grew in size and density as it moved toward the company along the horizon. The wood fire that produced the huge clouds was moving on the river.

"It's that new, steam-driven boat we saw tied up at the New Orleans wharf," a man behind William shouted.

"One of the deck hands said the boat was just like the one that man Fulton built in New York," another man yelled. "I've got to see this," and he raced for the river melting into the trees to reach the river bank. In an instant, the whole company had filtered through the trees to see the steamboat.

Out on the river the big, white boat ploughed through the current going north toward Baton Rouge. Silhouetted behind the deck railings were men in top hats and frock coats and women in bonnets and full skirts that tilted and fluttered in the air moved by their passage.

The militia men shouted and waved, a few shot their rifles in the air, the steam whistle blasted its response, and the passengers waved back. A celebration of the advanced technology in river travel created a joyous occasion. The boat moved on beyond the gawkers on the bank, not slowing its speed by the encounter.

Watching the boat complete the bend in the river and grow smaller, Jock, James, and William stood together. Only its rear was now visible. The big stern-wheel turned the water to white foam leaving a long trail as it pushed the boat away.

"I bet Old Hickory would have liked to have had two or three of those with cannons mounted on the front decks when the British fleet sailed up the river. He could have driven those British back to England without the battle we fought," James said.

"Now dat would be de way to travel up river. Tak'n it easy on de deck. Relax'n in de sunshine. Dat's fer me," said Jock, turning to return to the road.

"How much do you think it would cost to ride that boat home?" James asked.

"That's fer rich folk, not fer de likes of us," Jock replied.

"It will take a lot more gold than we will ever see," William said.

Sam and Mathew, standing next to James, said they had gone to the docks to see this boat. One of the boat's crew had told them it had been built by a Pittsburgh company in Brownsville, Pennsylvania, south of Pittsburgh. They used the same plans that Robert Fulton had used. The steamboat sailed down the Ohio River to the Mississippi, then up to St. Louis, then down to New Orleans. Now, it was making the return trip. The Pittsburgh company had built two of these boats and was working on a third.

After the steamboat disappeared, the company reassembled on the road ready to continue their march north.

"Alright, you've had your break now. We lost a lot of time with your lollygagging, so let's pick up the pace," the lieutenant shouted. Men grumbled. What was the rush? We've got time to get back to Tennessee before our enlistments run out.

As the march progressed, Maria returned to William's thoughts. *He wanted to be with her; how could she not want the same? His chest ached and he knew he was in love with her. He had to go back to find her. He needed to talk to Captain Stewart.*

The company had walked for over two miles from the steamboat sighting. He told Jock and James that he had to go back and try to talk to Maria. He was going to ask the Captain for permission to leave the march and go back.

Both Jock and James objected and explained again that she had rejected him. Her disappearance from the balcony, from the Tavern, and in the message the old, black woman brought him--all had been strong ways of saying she did not wish to see him again.

"I know, but I love her. She has to tell me herself," he said in reply to their arguments. "I've got to try one more time."

William moved forward to the lieutenant for permission to talk to the Captain who was at the head of the column.

"No, get back in line," the lieutenant stated flatly. "You can talk to the Captain when we stop for midday meal. I heard what you were saying about some girl back there. She'll wait for you if she's interested in you. Now get back in line."

William slipped back to his place next to Jock and James. *He was hurt. Why wouldn't the lieutenant let him talk to the Captain? The lieutenant was being mean for no good reason. Anger began to grow in him. This didn't make sense. What had he done to the lieutenant to be treated this way?* William said as much to his friends and some of the other men.

Both Jock and James and the other men agreed that the lieutenant was being unreasonable. All we were doing was walking home. There was no urgency. William could go back, talk to the girl, and return by night camp the next day at the latest.

The lieutenant could hear the grumbling and came back to see what was going on.

"Let William go see the Captain," one of the men said.

"No, he stays with the column. I don't want to lose any men to fantasy ideas. He stays here and that's an end of it," the lieutenant snapped.

Jock said, stepping over to the lieutenant, "I'm not in yer Army. Ye can't order me around. I will go see de Captain and explain William's request and yer refusal."

The lieutenant didn't like this attitude and spouted out, "You're traveling with us. That puts you under my orders. Now, get back in line!"

"I don't think so, and I don't think ye can make me." With that Jock bellowed, "Captain Stewart, may we talk to ye, Sir?"

At the head of the column, Captain Stewart heard the call. He had been hearing increasingly loud voices from behind him and was just about to send the sergeant back to learn what was happening. He stepped to the side allowing the column to pass him. He waited for Jock, the lieutenant, and William to reach his position then he continued walking with them.

"What's this all about, Lieutenant?" the Captain asked.

The lieutenant quickly explained William's request to see the Captain about leaving the company and returning to New Orleans to find some girl he'd seen, then mentioned his denial of William's request, and Jock's interference.

"Is this the girl you have been trying to find for the past few days, William?" the Captain asked.

"Yes, Captain, I saw her watching us march out of town. She was on the balcony of the last big house we passed. I've just got to go back and talk to her. I love her. I've got to know why she has hidden from me. What she is afraid of?" William replied.

"I saw a young woman watching us from the balcony as we passed. She was very attractive. I also saw those two men at the other end of the balcony. They didn't look friendly at all. The taller of the two looked familiar. I couldn't put a name to him; however, I don't believe he has a good reputation. Jock, would you go with William if I let him go?"

Jock replied, "if William would like some company, I will go with him."

"I would like to go, too," James joined in.

"I would like to have Jock and James with me," William said.

"Alright, William, I will give you permission to return to New Orleans to find your girl. But you must be back with the company at Baton Rouge. We are to march up the River road to Tennessee. It will take us three days to reach Baton Rouge, so that is how much time you have. If you fail to catch up at Baton Rouge, you will be marked *Absent Without Leave* which brings a very serious penalty. Do you understand?" the Captain asked.

"I understand," William said.

"James, that wound in your shoulder has not completely healed. You better stay with us where you can get medical attention," said the Captain.

"Jock, you are not under my command, so you can come and go as you please. William, I suggest you get your bed rolls from the supply wagons and maybe some provisions," the Captain recommended.

"Thank you very much, Captain. We will catch up at Baton Rouge." With that William and Jock waited beside the road for the supply wagons. Quickly they got their gear and some food for three days and started back for New Orleans.

The Captain and the lieutenant watched them go. "That's the last we'll see of them, Captain," said the lieutenant. "It's a fool's errand if you ask me."

"They will be back. I know William. He's a good, young man, and Jock will go wherever William goes. Jock is certainly capable, and he will protect William," the Captain emphasized, as he turned to return to the front of the column.

The lieutenant watched the distant figures; they were jogging now. He shook his head and resumed the march.

Chapter Seven

Forest Moods

Weather in Louisiana could be cold, and on this day the air cooled their faces even when the sun reached its zenith. The sun felt warm but not hot. The road William and Jock were following was wide enough for wagons with a man walking alongside. Its hard-packed-dirt surface did not give any comfort to the feet of the jogging men. There had been no rain for several days. Dust rose up from every step. The dust the company had stirred up when it marched by had settled on the bushes and trees that lined the roadway turning them a dusty gray.

Jock was not used to jogging for long periods. Very quickly he began to get winded. He didn't complain, but William noticed the big man's heavy breathing and slowed their pace to a fast walk. As anxious as he was to get back to the house where he had seen Maria, he was also aware of his friend's discomfort.

In the trees they could hear birds talking to each other. Conversation would make the time pass quicker and keep their minds from their fatigue.

"That's a mocking bird," William told Jock as one particular birdcall reached their ears. "The mocking bird has a lot of different calls. At night during mating season, you can hear the male as he tries to attract a female. They chirp all night long sometimes. You don't want one outside your window when you go to bed. They'll keep you awake."

The song stopped, and a light, gray bird with dark, gray wings that had white markings flew from a perch in a tree beside the road. It landed in a tree ahead of them. The flight was jerky. A few flaps of the wings, glide, more flaps, glide, resulting in an up down flight. Its tail would spread and fold as it flew.

"There's that noisy bird," William said, as the bird flew into another tree seemingly to keep in front of them. The song began again. There were other birds around as they moved down the road. A bright streak of yellow flew across the road.

"I think that is a flycatcher," William told Jock.

"Do ye know a lot about birds, William?" Jock asked.

"I know some. My knowledge is from watching them in the forests back home. My father and mother have told me some of the birds' names. There are birds around our farm such as sparrows, wrens, and swallows that eat the insects. And, of course, the mocking birds are there, too," said William.

A movement in the sky caught his eye as a hawk floated slowly around making large circles in the air; his checkered, creamy, white belly and wings were clearly visible against the blue sky.

"There's a hawk looking for supper," William told Jock. "They eat mice and other small animals. When they can catch a pigeon or other small bird, they will eat it, as well."

Jock nodded without answering, thinking and watching the hawk. After a pause that lasted several minutes, he asked, "William, will ye teach me about de birds and de forest? Also, I'd like to know how to hunt and find roots and plants dat can be eaten. I have lived on a ship most of my life. I know very little about how to live on land. I would like very much to know about farms and living in de woods, fer example, how to walk quietly through dry leaves."

"I'd be happy to teach you what I know. We can start right now," William replied to his friend.

As they walked along, William explained about the birds of the forest. He told of sitting motionless in the woods, listening to the sounds of birds and animals.

"The forest is full of sounds," William said. "Each one is unique. When one listens, remains unmoving and quiet, the animals come out. The birds land near to you. Birds can tell you of someone or something being close by. A bird will watch someone trying to hide. If you watch the birds and listen to their sounds, they will tell you much about what is going on in the forest."

"Leaves falling from the trees have distinct sounds, so do dead twigs and larger branches when they fall. The sound of a mouse or chipmunk scurrying across a bed of leaves is quite different from a fox or raccoon crossing the same bed of leaves."

William told Jock of the moods of the forest in the seasons of the year. Jock listened intently and asked questions when something was not clear. They were moving along at a good pace. The morning passed into afternoon.

Chapter Eight

Blue Belle

The two men came to the plantation the company had passed earlier. Several horses were grazing in a field surrounded by a white-washed fence. William's appraising eye quickly picked out the plow horses from the riding horse and the wagon horses. He began explaining the differences to Jock.

"If we had a horse and wagon, dis trip would be a lot easier and faster," Jock suggested.

"You're right, Jock, but I don't have enough money to buy or even rent a horse and wagon." William realized that Jock had said wagon not two horses. Apparently, Jock did not know how to ride a horse.

"How much would it cost to buy a horse and wagon?" Jock asked.

"I don't know, maybe as much as $50.00 for a good horse and another $50.00 for a wagon and harness," William replied.

"Good, I've got some money. Let's see if dis farmer will sell us a horse and wagon," said Jock, pointing toward the farm house. They could see a man standing on the porch of the house watching them. Jock waved at the man as they started up the path toward the house.

The man seemed leery of them because they were carrying rifles slung over their shoulders. A shotgun leaned against the wall of the house near the man. He picked it up and held it across his chest in a non-threatening manner.

"Hello, Sir," William said, as they came close enough to be heard. "We are from the company of soldiers that passed here a while back. May we approach and talk with you?" Waiting for an invite to advance into the man's front yard, they stopped. William had spotted a black man at the side of the house with a musket. He was trying to stay out of sight and still keep an eye on the two men.

"You deserters from your company?" the man asked still suspicious. His speech carried what William believed to be a French accent.

"No," William said respectfully, "we are returning to New Orleans on an errand for a couple of days. Because it's a long walk, we thought we might rent a horse and wagon for the trip. Would you have a horse and wagon you could rent to us?"

"I don't have any horses to rent, but if you got some cash money, there is one I might sell you," the man said. "As for a wagon, there's only my farm wagon. I can't sell it. However, I do have my son's old sulky. You can fix it to carry two men, although he's a might big for a sulky," he observed, pointing at Jock.

The horse turned out to be a sorrel mare about fourteen or fifteen years old. She had been used to pull the sulky. The man admitted the horse was good, but she was getting too old to train for the plow. The horse would get them wherever they wanted to go, and she could move along at a trot for long periods at a time.

After some haggling, they agreed on a price for the

horse, the sulky, and some used harness. Jock paid the man the agreed price from his small bag of coins. The farmer allowed Jock to use some of his tools to fashion a double seat replacing the sulky's old single seat.

The farmer's wife had come out of the house accompanied by a young boy about ten years old after the farmer had asked the black man to bring the horse around. William and Jock had introduced themselves to the man when they started discussing the horse. The wife offered them something to eat and drink. They had not stopped to eat, and they were hungry. They readily accepted her offer. The boy watched as the big man prepared the sulky. As the boy became more comfortable, he began asking questions. He was full of questions about the Army and the Battle with the British. William answered as best he could.

The food was good, and the lemon drink she served with the bread and meat was cold and not too sweet.

When Jock finally got the sulky's seat ready and William had the mare in harness and hitched to the sulky, they had been there over an hour. William's anxiety had increased with the delay, so he quickly climbed aboard. Jock followed.

"You boys can sell that horse and sulky when you get where you are going," and with that the farmer handed Jock a bill of sale.

"Thank you for your help. We really appreciate the food. Thank you. Goodbye," said William, as he started the horse down the path to the road then turned toward New Orleans at a trot. The farmer, his wife and boy waved. Jock waved back as the road side trees enveloped them.

William was anxious. He knew they had spent way too much time getting the horse and sulky. It would be late afternoon before they reached Maria's house.

The horse proved to be better than William had

expected, and the road disappeared under her hooves. The horse's name was Blue Belle. She seemed to want to move at a faster pace than the trot, so William let her run for about a mile then slowed her to let her catch her breath. They were making up the lost time.

Jock held on as tight as he could. His knuckles turned white. He wasn't used to riding behind a fast horse. In fact, he wasn't used to riding at all.

Chapter Nine

The City House

The sun had dropped low in the sky when Blue Belle pulled the sulky into the circular driveway in front of the house where William had seen Maria. The sun would set in about an hour. He got off of the sulky and rubbed his rear-end. It hurt from bouncing around on the wooden seat.

Jock got down, also rubbing his behind as he remarked emphatically, "I don't know which is worse running all the way here or riding that thing. Before we ride it much more, we're getting some seat padding."

William tied Blue Belle to the hitching post and walked up the steps to the front door. He found the bell chain and pulled it. There was no owner's name beside the door. *Did Maria live here or had she been visiting? How should he begin? All the way here he had been thinking about an opening statement or reason for being at the front door. Maybe he should just ask for Maria and see what happened from there.* He pulled the chain again and waited.

Several more tries still did not produce a response.

He tried the door handle. It was locked. The drapes were pulled across all of the front windows, but he tried to find a crack to see in. The one opening he did find showed the interior as dark. There had been people here with Maria. Where were they now? Why didn't someone answer the front door?

William stood still trying to understand. Suddenly, the hairs on the back of his neck stood up. His instincts told him that he was being watched. Moving only his eyes, he checked the windows. No one looked out at him. Slowly, he turned to the North and saw nothing. He turned his gaze to the South. A large, old, black man stood at the corner of the house. He wore oversized work pants held up by suspenders and a dress shirt--its best days were obviously years ago. The old man's feet were bare.

"What you want, young master?" The old man asked. Not waiting for an answer, he continued, "All gone, no one here, house all closed up, not be back for a long time." The old man muttered in a flat tone, but there was an edge of nervousness in his voice.

Did this man know William? There seemed to be something familiar about him, but William could not recollect ever seeing him before.

"Where'd they go?" William asked.

"They go away, up river," the old man answered.

William started toward him. "Did Maria go up river?" he asked. "I want to talk to Maria."

The old man's eyes widened for an instant. He knew Maria. William stopped in front of the old man who nervously adjusted his weight from leg-to-leg. Still, he stood his ground. When Jock walked up beside William, the old man could not stand still.

"You go away. Don't come back," he said, and turned to leave.

William took hold of the old man's arm, preventing

him from walking away.

"Please sir, let me go," the old man pleaded. "I don't know nothing: Master Manuel will kill you if you hurt me."

"I won't hurt you if you tell me what I need to know; otherwise, I'll turn him loose on you," William said, indicating the huge man beside him. "Who is your master? Manuel?"

The old man was scared, but his voice didn't waver when he replied, "Master Manuel and he'll whip me if I talk to you. Master Manuel owns this place. He owns me. He is very important man. He told me not to talk to anyone. I can't talk to you. You must go away."

William felt bad for the old man. He was obviously very much afraid of his owner. William softened his tone some and loosened his grip on the old man's arm.

"We won't hurt you. Your master will never hear from us about the information you are going to give us. We are Maria's friends. We only want to talk to her."

The old man remained unconvinced. He repeated, "She go up river. I don't know nothing. You go away."

William and Jock exchanged glances. Maria had been here, and now she had gone up river, presumably, with the two men they had seen on the balcony and the older woman. The old man knew more than he admitted. They needed to find a way to get him to talk about Maria.

William decided to try another tactic.

"Can you show us inside the house? If no one is at home as you say, then no one will know we have been here. No one can tell your master. We won't touch anything. It is a beautiful house. The gardens in front and the water fountain make a very nice picture. Maybe, we will buy it," giving the old man an excuse for their going inside.

"You can say we insisted on seeing the inside, and you could not stop us."

The old man thought about this.

"The house is all closed up. There is nothing to see. The furniture is all covered."

William stepped around the old man and started toward the back of the house.

"Is this the way into the house from the back?" William knew the front door was locked.

Running after William, the old man frantically yelled, "Oh no, you can't go back there."

"Yes, we can," William replied, and continued to the corner of the house. As he rounded into the back area, he saw a well-manicured lawn and garden with several chairs and a bench. On one side was a good-sized barn which could house four or more horses and a carriage. The big, double doors on the front of the barn were partially open. The barn was dark inside and appeared to be empty. Farther back behind the barn, he could see three shacks that were probably servant quarters.

"Maybe your master is coming back," William said motioning to the open barn doors.

"No, they all go up river," the old man repeated. "I just putting the lawn furniture into the barn so they will be out of the weather. I am the caretaker. I take care of everything. I wait for Master Manuel to return. See I have a pass," he said, producing a piece of paper from his pocket and handing it to William. William read the poorly scribbled message out loud for Jock to hear:

To whoever needs to know, the bearer of this pass is Ben, my slave. He is the caretaker of my house and property and is trusted by me. He is to live on my property with my permission.

Signed,

Manuel Olivarez

William handed the paper back to the old man. Maybe now he had Maria's last name, "Olivarez."

"We will go inside now, Ben, before we lose the

light." William said, as he walked toward the back door followed by the, still-protesting, old man and Jock.

William pushed open the back door and stepped inside. He had entered into a large kitchen. Working at the sink cleaning some pots stood the old, black woman who had handed Maria's letter to him where he waited in the park. At the sound of William's footsteps, she turned and saw him. She jumped, let out a little cry and froze. Fear replaced the look of recognition on her face. The old man came in behind William, followed by Jock. Seeing her husband, the old woman's eyes shifted to the old man, but she said nothing.

"I know you," William exclaimed. "You're Maria's servant. You brought her message to me. Where is Maria?"

The old woman was thunderstruck. Her knees buckled, and she collapsed to the floor, praying hysterically not to be hurt and killed.

Jock moved around William, knelt by the old woman saying softly, "we're not going to hurt ye, grandmother. We need to know about Maria. We know she is in trouble," he explained, trying the thought that they knew more than had been told.

"We would like to help if we can," and with that, Jock gently picked up the old woman. He placed her in a chair then took a step back.

Almost panic-stricken, the old woman searched the faces of each of the men for help and tried hard to make herself appear smaller. Her eyes were wide and her hands were clasped on her chest. Her whole body seemed to tremble with fear.

William watched the old woman for a minute. He turned to Ben who now stood beside the old woman.

"I know you, now. You drove that big, black carriage that I saw around the park. Without your livery uniform and in those old clothes, you fooled me," William recalled.

"You drove Maria to the park to meet me and to the tavern to dance. You were there to protect and chaperone her. And you drove this woman," he said, pointing at the old woman, "to deliver Maria's message to me."

Ben was trapped. Slowly, he nodded his assent. He could not lie. He leaned over the old woman and said, "Sarah, these men are not here to hurt us. The young one is the man Miss Maria likes so much. You gave him Miss Maria's message in the park. Our Maria tried to protect him from Master Manuel and Master Hernandez. Sarah, our baby is in trouble; you know it and I know it. These young masters have guessed it. Old Miss Olivia would want us to help our Maria if we can. You and I cannot help her now, but maybe they can."

The old woman silently watched William intently. Then in a small voice, she asked, "Do you really want to help my baby?"

"Yes, very much. I love Maria," William replied.

"Who is Manuel Olivarez?" Jock asked.

"He is our owner, so he says. Old Miss Olivia gave us to Miss Maria to take care of her as we have done all of her life. But Master Manuel says women can't own slaves, so he be our master."

"Who is Miss Olivia?" William gently questioned.

"Miss Olivia is their mother. She lives on the plantation El Hermoso Lugar. In English it means *The Beautiful Place*. Miss Olivia is old and not well. She cannot help Maria," Ben replied.

"Master Manuel is Miss Maria's older brother."

William, feeling a bit more trusted, bravely ventured, "Where are they now?"

"They all went up river," Ben repeated. "All four. Señor Hernandez, Master Manuel, Miss Maria and Señora Elizabeth, Miss Maria's chaperone. They all go to St. Louis on the steamboat."

William felt a pain in his chest. That woman had been Maria that he had seen on the steamboat this morning. Of course, she had been too far away for him to recognize. There had been two women on the boat's deck. They must have been Maria and Señora Elizabeth.

Dang it, he thought. *That boat is probably to Baton Rouge by now or beyond. Even on a fast horse he knew he couldn't catch it. Blue Belle is too old and could never go that distance not even at a trot. He decided he better learn as much as he could about the Olivarez's family, at least as much as Ben and Sarah would tell him.*

Ben interrupted William's thoughts. "There is something else we need to tell you. Master Manuel knows about you. His henchman, Ortega, saw Miss Maria dance in the tavern for you and then sit beside you at your table. Master Manuel was very angry. Ortega is a very dangerous man with a knife or gun. He and his friend Chavez have done some very bad things for Master Manuel. You must be very careful. After you marched past this morning and shouted at Maria (Yes, I saw you.), Master Manuel sent me to find Ortega. I think Master Manuel wants you killed."

"What does Ortega look like?" Jock asked.

"He is thin and short, with a narrow face, a big, crooked nose, black eyes and hair. He is a bad man, and he is smart. He usually wears brown leather clothes. Chavez, Ortega's henchman, is larger and more muscular and dresses the same. They are almost always together, unless one or the other is reporting in to Manuel," Ben finished.

"Ortega sounds like de man I saw leaving de tavern while ye were talking to Maria in de courtyard. Too bad we didn't catch him," Jock said.

"Miss Maria told me she had seen Ortega in the tavern," Ben said. "I was frightened for her because I knew Ortega would go straight to Master Manuel and tell

77

what he had seen. Master Manuel was waiting for Maria when we returned to this house. He was very angry."

"Miss Maria faced up to him saying she would do as she pleased and there was nothing he could do about that. Master Manuel hit her and knocked her to the floor. He said he would not have his sister dancing in a tavern and cavorting with the low-life that hangs around taverns. He ordered Señora Elizabeth not to let Maria out of her sight and stormed out."

"After Master Manuel left, Miss Maria ordered me to get the carriage. She and Señora Elizabeth were going to the plantation to see her mother. I drove them out there immediately."

William felt his blood begin to boil. "Señor Manuel will pay when I catch up to him."

"Dat explains Maria's running away, de note, and den hiding today," Jock said.

"What is this Señor Hernandez to Maria? Does he know of Maria's dancing or meeting me?" William asked.

"No," Ben replied. "Señor Hernandez is very rich, *and* he is Miss Maria's fiancé. Master Manuel would not want him to know because he might lose him as a future brother-in-law."

A small clock on the kitchen wall announced the hour with five chimes. Soon it would be dark.

Chapter Ten

Family Story

As dusk deepened the shadows in the kitchen, Ben lit two oil lamps casting a warm light on the cabinet-lined walls. A large, wood-burning, stove occupied the wall next to the back door. An orange-red glow peeked through a small opening in the stove's face. Steam rose from the large, copper kettle above the fire. On the counter next to the large sink stood a small iron pump.

Sarah had neither moved from her chair, nor had she said anything more after asking William about his wanting to help Maria.

William pulled a chair in front of Sarah and sat down. Jock leaned against the center table. Ben also brought a chair to sit beside Sarah and took her hand to reassure her.

"Ben, Sarah, please continue telling us about this confrontation between Maria and Manuel," William requested.

"Did Manuel follow Maria to the plantation?"

"Yes, the next afternoon Master Manuel arrived at the plantation," Ben related. "His anger had cooled considerably, and he apologized for hitting Maria. Then he announced that they would be joining Señor Hernandez on his trip to St. Louis. They would be traveling on the new steamboat that had just arrived in New Orleans. He told Miss Maria and Señora Elizabeth to pack for a long journey. He ordered them to return to the city house in two days."

"Miss Olivia objected to the trip but was overruled by her son. So, I drove Miss Maria and Señora Elizabeth back here two days later. That was the day Miss Maria wrote the note and sent Sarah and me to deliver it."

"Tell us about Maria's family, her brother, and Señor Hernandez," William encouraged.

Over the next thirty minutes the couple recounted the history of the Olivarez's family.

Maria's grandfather had come to New Orleans as a Captain in the Spanish Army. Because of his rank and his family's political influence, he was able to bring his wife to New Orleans. They liked New Orleans and decided to make their home there. The Captain resigned from the Army and started a trading company. They had three children: Maria's father, the oldest, and two daughters.

The youngest daughter, Miss Elizabeth, had married a prominent New Orleans merchant. When her husband passed away a few years ago, she moved in with her brother to become Maria's chaperone. The other sister, when she was of age decided to visit their family in Spain, but her ship sank in a hurricane. No one survived.

Maria's father grew up in New Orleans and joined his father's trading firm. Eventually, he took over and grew the business into a very prosperous company. While a young gentleman, he went to the theater often. It was there he met Maria's mother. She was a member of a dance troupe touring from Spain. He courted her, and they were married. Manuel came first, then five-years-and-a-few-months later Pedro arrived. Maria followed two years

80

later. Maria was seven-and-a-half years younger than Manuel. Both his father and his mother spoiled him because he was first born. They gave him anything he wanted. His father refused to discipline him. His mother tried, but was not backed up by his father. As a result, Manuel became willful, demanding, and often hard to control. A display of temper usually earned whatever he wished.

Pedro's arrival resulted in Manuel no longer being the center of attention. This second child made Manuel's behavior worse. He greatly resented the attention given to Pedro. He showed his resentment at every opportunity. His parents tried to give him as much of their time as they could, but Pedro was not healthy and constantly needed their care.

Jealous of all the attention Pedro received, Manuel became a disappointment to his parents. His mother and father could not understand his resentment of his brother. After all he was the oldest and with that comes responsibility and the expectation that he would help look after his brother. He should understand his brother's needs. His parents explained to him that he was not being neglected. They loved him just as much as before Pedro came. It was simply that Pedro's health needs required a lot of their parents' time.

When Maria came, Manuel did not resent her. She was a girl and not competition. Girls must be protected and sheltered. She would not compete with him for his parents' attention.

Maria grew into a strong, healthy little girl. As she got bigger it became obvious that she would be independent with a mind of her own. However, she loved her brothers and never hesitated to show them her feelings.

When Pedro was about four-and-a-half-years old, he and his sister were playing in Maria's second floor bedroom. Their ever-present nanny left them alone to help another servant with a brief chore on the first floor. The nanny asked Manuel, who was studying his lessons in his room, to watch the children. Pedro, perhaps looking for the nanny, wandered out of the bedroom.

The nanny and staff heard the fall and Pedro's yelling. They rushed to the stairs. Manuel was standing at the top of the stairs looking down. Pedro's fall had resulted in a broken arm and a small bruise on the side of his head. No other injuries were apparent. Ben had been sent to get the doctor.

After setting the arm, the doctor examined the bruise, and because the boy seemed fine, dismissed it. The boy complained only of the arm. About three hours later the boy began screaming that his head hurt, and then he curled up on his bed. He went into a coma. The doctor returned and examined the boy, but could not find the problem. Never regaining consciousness, Pedro died of his injuries three days later.

His parents were devastated. Manuel seemed uninterested.

Manuel's father asked Manuel if he had seen his brother fall. Did he see what happened?

"No, I was in my room reading. Pedro had said he tripped. That must be what happened," Manuel replied.

Maria, unperturbed by the noise of the fall, had continued playing in her bedroom. Pedro's crying, however, brought her to the stairs to stand beside Manuel to watch Pedro being carried to his room. She stayed by Pedro's side, trying as a two-year old might, to help her brother. Pedro's injury upset her. His arm hurt and he cried. His coma she didn't understand. She kept asking why Pedro would not awake from his nap and play with her.

Under strange and suspicious circumstances, Pedro had died when Maria was just two.

With Pedro gone, Manuel expected to again be the center of attention. This did not happen. Both mother and father seemed to be less interested in the boy. Their grief over Pedro's death was deep and consuming. They expected Manuel, now eleven years old, to be more grown up and mature. They expected him to understand their grief and be less demanding as they adjusted to Pedro's death. His mother hugged him and told him how much she loved him, but this affection apparently was not enough!

Manuel's father tried to impress him with the importance of studying hard so he could eventually take over the family business. Manuel did not like studying and remained an average student. His parents decided to send him to the best private school in New Orleans for a better education and some badly needed discipline.

The school believed in training the body, as well as, the mind, so he was taught how to use a sword, shoot a pistol, and fight with his fists. He liked the sword and the pistol and became proficient with both weapons. Since he did not like the personal contact of fist fighting, he did not master this part of the self-defense training.

It was in school that he met Fernando Hernandez. Fernando was two years ahead of Manuel. Older boys were assigned a younger boy to advise and support, which was one of the traditions of the school. Fernando became Manuel's mentor. Almost immediately, Fernando exerted his influence over Manuel. In return, Manuel idealized Fernando and followed unquestioning wherever Fernando led.

Fernando was the only child of a wealthy plantation family. His mother died giving him life. His father was elderly and could not handle the boy. A white nanny was hired to help raise and educate him. This helped for a while because she treated him like a son. But he had a temper. Anger would rise quickly in him to the point of violence at any real or imagined insult. His father paid little attention to Fernando, blaming him for taking his beloved wife's life.

Fernando was a top student. He understood that knowledge obtained from books would be very valuable in the future. But he also learned about gambling. He liked playing cards for money and became quite good. Often he won the allowances of other boys.

When two boys his age refused to play cards with him, he became very angry. He picked a fight with the larger of the boys and beat him badly. As a result of the fight, Fernando was asked to leave the school.

Several years later Fernando challenged that boy to a duel and killed him. Manuel was his second. Fernando has been in many duels since then.

Manuel believed he must protect Maria and make decisions for her. Acting under this belief, he has promoted her engagement to Fernando. He believed that it was in her best interests to marry Fernando. Maria loved her brother, but she did resent his domineering ways.

From the first time Fernando saw Maria dance at the age of twelve, he became infatuated with her. She was beautiful even then and showed promise of being one of the most beautiful women in New Orleans. He knew from that time on he must have her. He continually promoted this idea to Manuel. Manuel thought the merger of the two families through this union would be in the best interest of both families and promised Maria's hand. Miss Olivia said Maria could not be married until she was eighteen. Manuel could not change this, so Fernando agreed to wait.

Fernando spent whatever time he could visiting the Olivarez home and talking with Maria. Excitedly, she told him of the future she planned for herself. She told of her dreams of becoming a great dancer and of attending *La Academia de National* in Madrid to study dance as her mother had done. Fernando has promised to take her to Spain and to help her become a dancer.

"I do not think Señor Hernandez will keep his promise," Ben had said.

When Maria's father died, the prosperous business he had built came under the management of Manuel. The business immediately began to decline. Once good customers did not want to deal with the arrogant Manuel and took their business to his competitors. He tried intimidation to keep customers by using men like Ortega and Chavez with limited success.

Manuel also began spending money on gambling, drinking, and womanizing. The family business continued to decline until Manuel turned to Fernando for help. Because of Fernando's desire for Maria, he agreed to buy half the business and assume its management. Now, under Fernando's control and leadership, it was beginning to turn around.

"Manuel had become less and less involved with the company, but he continually drew off the profits. Fernando's desire for Maria was Manuel's hold on Fernando. However, I think there is something else that Manuel holds over Fernando," Ben concluded.

William stood up and stretched. He had a lot to ponder.

Chapter Eleven

The Staircase

William picked up one of the oil lamps and walked through the open door at the end of the kitchen. He held the lamp high to illuminate the room. A white, cotton cloth covered the long table that stretched into the darkness. Along the walls, white cloths also covered the chairs and sideboards. The lamp's light flickered sending ghostly shadows chasing around the room.

He heard Sarah ask Jock if he was hungry. Jock said he was always hungry. She offered to fix something for them and he accepted.

William walked the length of the room and passed under a good-sized-arched doorway into a spacious entrance hall. The front door had a dark stain with a shell-shaped design carved around a covered peephole. He continued across the hall into the parlor. His footfalls on the shiny wood floor created eerie echoes.

As in the dining room the furniture had been covered with white cloths. He could tell from what he could see under the cloths that the furniture was heavy and dark.

This, he guessed, to be the Spanish style of the time and probably expensive.

There were several rugs rolled up against one wall. Light rectangle and oval patches of wood floor showed where the rugs had been. There were built-in shelves to one side of a large fireplace. One of the shelves held some books. William walked over and read their titles. Four were in Spanish; the others were in English. He did not recognize any of the titles or authors. He returned to the hall.

Jock came up beside him and let out a low whistle.

"Dis is some place. I've never seen anything like it," he said.

"Yes, it is," responded William.

A long, curved staircase leading to the second floor leaned against one wall. The steps were polished wood matching the floor. The banisters were also polished wood, but the supporting posts had been lathed into an interesting, round design and painted white. The contrast was striking and pleasing to the eye.

Jock's carpenter's appreciation of fine woodwork came out as he began studying the staircase.

"Look at this, William," Jock noticed, pointing at two posts four steps up from the first floor. "Dose posts have been cut in a different pattern from de others. De original posts were broken out by a very hard blow. See how de wood where de posts fit into de step is splintered and ripped away. When de broken posts were replaced, de splinter holes were filled with light-colored putty. Dis was not a good carpentry job."

"I wonder what broke the original posts. Let's ask Ben," William suggested.

Just then, Ben entered the hall, summoning them to dinner. Jock asked about the two posts. Ben said that Masters Manuel and Fernando had some noisy parties with gambling and women. It was after one of those parties that he found the broken posts. He didn't know how they were broken because neither he nor Sarah were allowed in the house during those parties. But he thought something bad had happened because Manuel had awakened him in the middle of the night after a party and ordered him to hitch up the carriage and bring it to the back door. Manuel said that he would drive the carriage and Ben was told to return to his cabin.

From a crack in the door, Ben had watched Manuel and Fernando load an unconscious woman into the carriage and drive away. Manuel returned alone the next day. He ordered Ben to repair the broken stairway posts and *never* to tell anyone.

Ben led the way back to the kitchen now brightly lit with several lamps. A small table near the door had been set with silver table-ware on a red calico cloth. They sat down and the old woman brought each a steaming dish of stew. Fresh bread in individual baskets sat in front of each place. Also, a dish with butter and a decanter of red wine were on the table.

William and Jock were hungry and quickly devoured the feast. Jock had a second helping, telling Sarah how much he enjoyed her cooking. William asked if she had enough stew for the old couple and was assured that they had plenty to eat.

When they had eaten their fill, William asked about Miss Olivia. Ben told him that she was a good mistress and treated her slaves kindly. When Maria's father had been alive, they often entertained in this house. After he passed away a few years ago, Miss Olivia retired to the plantation. Now, she rarely came into the city. She preferred living in the country and seeing to the affairs of the plantation.

"Ben, we would like to meet Miss Olivia. Will you take us?" William asked.

The old man hesitated about a trip to the plantation,

but some gentle coaxing by William brought a reluctant agreement to visit Miss Olivia the next day.

The old man suggested that William and Jock stay the night in the barn. He did not think it appropriate for them to stay in the house. William agreed. After they finished eating, they thanked the old couple, telling them it was the best food they'd eaten in a long, long time. Sarah tried to hide the pleasure the compliment gave her.

Ben lit a lantern and led the way to the barn. In one of the stalls, Blue Belle stood munching on some hay. The sulky had been rolled to the rear of the barn with the harness draped over the seat, and their rifles and gear were beside one of its wheels.

The old man had done this at some time during the evening.

"I thought it best," explained Ben, "to bring your horse and rig back here before someone got too curious about it and started asking what you were doing here."

"That was a good idea," William replied.

"There is fresh hay up in the loft," Ben told them while hanging up the lantern. He said he would come for them in the morning and disappeared out the big doors closing them as he went.

Jock walked over to Blue Belle and began rubbing her head affectionately. Liking the attention, the horse nuzzled him.

William joined them. He picked up a handful of straw and began rubbing her down, as he whispered to her, "You did a good job for us today, old girl, and we appreciated it."

Early the next morning the big doors opened, and the old man stepped inside. He called to them saying that Sarah was fixing some breakfast. They could get washed up at the backyard pump. As they descended from the loft, Blue Belle greeted them with soft nickering. Jock went to her and rubbed her ears. He really liked this horse.

In the kitchen, the table was set as the night before. Eggs fried with some bacon and fresh bread waited. Again, Sarah proved to be an excellent cook.

William was anxious to be on the way, so he hurried Jock along. They thanked Sarah again with praise for her cooking skills. She seemed embarrassed, for she was not used to receiving compliments for her work. She told them to go on and set about cleaning up while humming some ancient tune.

Ben had Blue Belle harnessed and ready. Jock took a board from the barn and made a third seat for the old man. He also found a couple of empty feed sacks and stuffed them with hay for the seat. They would be crowded, but all three could ride. The men climbed aboard and drove out onto the road.

William guided Blue Belle according to Ben's directions. They threaded their way through several streets to a ferry boat and crossed the Mississippi river. Once on the west bank, Ben steered them onto a road leading away from the river. The road, if it could be called that, was two dirt tracks with grass tufts in the middle. The old man explained that not many people lived out this direction from the city.

The road was surrounded by trees and in some places thick brush grew around them. The songs of birds could be heard over the sounds of Blue Belle's hooves. Once in a while the road would curve near a swampy area. At one large swamp, William saw what he thought was a big, fallen tree, but then it got up and walked on four, short legs into the water. William's jaw dropped open in disbelief.

"Dat's an alligator," Jock laughed, "a big one at dat. Maybe three-to-four-lengths long."

William had never seen any creatures like that. He had heard about them, and he was fascinated.

Jock read William's mind and explained, "dey're fierce and mean. Ye're food to dem. If dey get a hold on ye, ye're as good as dead because it is almost impossible to pry d'eir mouth open. De gators grab d'eir victims and pull dem under de water drowning dem. Den they stuff de hapless victim under some log or dead fall to be eaten later. Gators are nothing to fool around with. De swamps are full of dem."

As they traveled, Jock talked of his experiences going through the swamps and bayous from Barataria to New Orleans when delivering pirate loot to the Lafitte brothers' warehouse so the stolen goods could be sold.

Over an-hour-and-a-half after leaving New Orleans, they approached a large recently plowed field. On the far side of the field, they could see a good-sized white frame house with a porch that wrapped around three sides. There were several out buildings and a large barn. The old man said that this was plantation El Hermoso Lugar, Miss Olivia's home.

"The driveway to the house is just past the plowed field," Ben directed.

William turned Blue Belle into the lane leading to the house. As they approached, several people could be seen turning to watch the horse and cart carrying the three men drive up to the house. A handsome, older woman got up from her seat on the porch and walked to the head of the steps and watched them approach.

William brought Blue Bell to a stop at a black-iron hitching post. Ben hopped down from the cart and walked to the foot of the porch steps.

"Well, Ben, who have you brought to see us?" she asked. Her voice had a thick Spanish accent, and its tenor was one of authority.

"Mornin', Miss Olivia. These young gentlemen are friends of Miss Maria. They asked if they could meet you. They came to the house looking for Maria."

Miss Olivia folded her arms across her chest, turned her gaze on William and Jock and waited. William and Jock dismounted and stood beside Blue Belle. They did not approach the steps, choosing to wait for an invitation.

"So, you are Maria's friends. How did you come to know her?" Miss Olivia demanded. There was no nonsense in her tone.

"I thought I knew all of her friends and acquaintances. She is a very, sheltered, young lady and, therefore, has few friends."

Now it was William's turn. He had thought long and hard about what he would say to Maria's Mother. Finally, he decided to be straight forward and honest.

"Good Morning, Señora Olivarez. My name is William Russell, and this is my friend Jock Smith," indicating the big man. "We saw Maria dance and were captured by her grace and beauty," William said, leaving out the part about the Tavern.

"After her dance, Maria and I spent a couple of wonderful hours talking. Later she danced again then disappeared, promising to meet me in two days, so we could talk again. She did meet me, and we spent an amazing afternoon talking and laughing. She told me what a great dancer you were. We got along very well. I believe we liked each other very much." William spoke with respect and admiration of Maria's dancing skills.

"A few days later, we met again, and she danced for me, but an employee of your son frightened her. She left in a hurry but agreed to meet me two days later. However, she didn't meet me. This time she sent Sarah to give me a note that said she couldn't see me anymore and that it would be very dangerous for her and for me if I didn't do as she asked. Therefore, I have tried to find her to see if I could help with whatever danger she faced."

"However, yesterday, as my militia company was leaving New Orleans to return to Tennessee, I saw her on the balcony of your city house. She immediately hid. At first, I intended to continue home and accept her rejections. But, the more I thought about this, the less I felt I could leave without talking to her one more time. She would have to tell me herself to forget her and to go away, never to see her again."

"I received permission from my company commander to return to the city to find her." William continued. "My friend Jock decided to accompany me in my search. At your city house, we found Ben and Sarah. I persuaded Ben to bring me here to meet you."

"Young man, do you know the meaning of the word, 'No'?" Miss Olivia demanded.

"Yes, my apologies, Señora. But, I just need to hear it from her," William answered. "If I do, then I will go away and never bother her again."

"Alright you've met me. What is it that you want from me?"

"I was hoping you would be willing to tell me about Maria's difficulties. I understand Manuel is forcing an unwanted fiancé on her. Maria dreams of becoming a great dancer like you. She told me about her dreams and plans," William replied.

"What do you know about her situation?" Miss Olivia said, still not inviting William and Jock to join her on the porch.

Quickly, William explained about Maria's no-name secrecy and what Ben and Sarah had told him.

"I know that she does not like Señor Hernandez and does not want to marry him. I know that her brother, Manuel, is forcing his will on her, and I know that she is afraid of the people around him. I know that she is young and full of life. She wants to dance. I care for her very much, and I want to help her if I can," William concluded.

Chapter Twelve

Miss Olivia

The young man, standing in front of Miss Olivia, seemed sincere in his feelings about her daughter. Maria had confided that she had met a handsome, young soldier whom she really liked. He had fine plans for his future and would be a very good catch. But Manuel was involved and that could be bad for the young man although he looked like he could take care of himself. Certainly, his big friend appeared capable. Sadly, she knew her son to be prone to violence when he did not get his way. Manuel was not a good man.

Miss Olivia felt her caution beginning to evaporate. William's truthfulness was having a positive effect. Still, should she talk to him about her daughter and her son and the man who was betrothed to Maria? Miss Olivia did not like Fernando Hernandez. He had a bad reputation. However, he was helping Manuel keep the family trading business from failing. Fernando was from a good family, and he was rich. He could give Maria all those things that she could no longer afford.

Her plantation just barely supported itself and the city

house. If she could sell the city house, she might be able to send Maria to Spain to school. But, Manuel would not hear of such a sale or of Maria's leaving. He said the business would pay the expenses of the city house. So far, she had not seen a penny of support.

Manuel lived most of the time in the city house and went to business from there. He rarely came to the plantation anymore. He made Maria stay in the city as much as he could. Maria preferred to live on the plantation, except when the theater was open. She loved to go to plays and the opera. When entertaining troupes from Spain were in New Orleans, Maria would stay in the city and attend the performances.

Miss Olivia was still uncertain about telling family business to someone she had just met. She needed to know William better.

"Alright, young man, come up on the porch and bring your friend. We will sit and talk some. You can tell me about yourself."

"Ben," she said, "you take the horse and cart to the barn and give her a good brushing. She looks a little lathered. She might like some fresh hay, too." With that Miss Olivia walked back to her comfortable chair and sat down. She indicated another chair near her for William and one for Jock.

"Sadie, bring us something cool to drink," Miss Olivia called out.

From just inside the front door came a weak reply of, "Yes, Mum."

William and Jock climbed the steps and took the indicated seats.

"Alright, young man, tell me about yourself," Maria's Mother said.

Sadie emerged from the house carrying a tray with three glasses and a pitcher filled with a sweet, lemon drink. There, also, was a small plate with some cookies.

After pouring each of the glasses, she handed one to Miss Olivia and one to each of the men. Then she passed around the cookie plate. Miss Olivia did not take a cookie, but Jock and William each took two.

William told her about his parent's farm, about the crops they grew and, about the animals they raised. He talked about his Mother and Father and about how they had come into the Tennessee wilderness with his uncle and three other families to build a new life. He told of the Bounty land each of the men had received for their service in the American Revolutionary War. His uncle had started a trading post and freighting business. And his uncle had used twenty acres of his Bounty land to establish their village of Russellville.

William talked of his love for the forest and how he enjoyed hunting. "Sometimes," he said, "I just like to track an animal, not to kill for food, but just to get close to watch and learn its habits." He told her about the shooting matches he had entered. He was modest and did not brag about the ones he had won.

They talked for over two hours with Miss Olivia listening attentively and asking questions when appropriate.

"Well, I believe I know you better and it is lunch time. Will you and Mr. Smith join me for some lunch?" she asked.

"After lunch I always take a nap. This afternoon when I awake, Mr. Smith, you will tell me about yourself," she stated.

"Sadie, is lunch ready?"

"Yes, Mum," Sadie replied from just inside the front door.

They followed Miss Olivia into the house, entering into a good-sized hall with the dining room on the left and a large parlor on the right. A banister stairway went to the second floor. The rooms were not well lit. The air inside was cool and comfortable. The table in the dining room was set with three places, one at the head of the table and the other two on each side. Miss Olivia went to the table's head. William moved quickly to pull the chair out for her as his mother had taught him. When they were seated, Sadie brought a tureen of soup and a plate of corn bread. Cow butter was on the table.

Miss Olivia talked about the plantation and the problems of growing crops to support the farm. She had a foreman who helped, but he was getting up in years and had begun to slow down. He was a free black man and lived with his wife in a cabin behind the house. His children had all grown up and moved North looking for a better life. The conversation flowed easily. However, Miss Olivia never mentioned Maria or her son.

The lunch was quite good. The soup was filling, the stick-to-your-ribs kind with vegetables and rice. The warm corn bread was just the right accompaniment. When they had finished, Miss Olivia excused herself. William helped her with her chair, and she said they could look around the farm. With that she went up the stairs and into one of the rooms.

Chapter Thirteen

Plantation El Hermoso Lugar

Jock and William walked outside and down the front steps. When they were out of earshot of the house, Jock said, "We haven't learned anything about Maria or Manuel, but Miss Olivia now knows a lot about ye."

"Jock, I think she is trying to decide whether we are trustworthy and whether we really are Maria's friends. I think if we tell her whatever she wants to know, be as honest as we can, we can win her over."

"Alright, I'll play along," Jock agreed.

They wandered around the house toward the barn where Blue Belle was stabled. The horse nickered when she saw them and moved to the front of the stall putting her head over the gate for Jock to rub her neck, which he did energetically. In a corner of the barn stood the large, box-shaped, black carriage William had seen at the park.

Ben and another large black man were in the barn when they entered. Ben introduced him as Samuel, Miss Olivia's overseer. He greeted them without smiling.

"Is Miss Olivia taking her nap?" he asked. "Would you like to look around the plantation? If you would, Ben here can show you. I've got some work to do." With that he left the barn and headed toward a shack some distance away.

"He doesn't trust you. He thinks you might be like Señor Fernando or Master Manuel, just out for yourselves. He is afraid you might hurt Miss Olivia. He is very protective of her," Ben said. "As he gets to know you, he will learn better."

"Thank you for your vote of confidence, Ben," William replied. "We would like you to show us around the plantation. But first, let me take a look at that carriage. You drove Maria to our meetings in it and Sarah to deliver Maria's note. It always looked empty. The day I looked inside it was empty, or was it? What is its secret?"

Ben replied, "There are two secret compartments under the seats that are big enough to hide someone small like Sarah. The day you jumped on the carriage footstep and looked inside, Sarah had just hidden herself under the back seat. You scared her and me almost to death when you did that. I'm surprised Sarah didn't cry out in fear and give away her hiding place."

"Thank you, Ben. Now, we shall look over the farm," suggested William.

Ben led the way pointing out the sheds and cabins behind the barn and explained the function of each. They moved on to a large pasture where six horses were grazing--two mares, two geldings, and two large draft horses. The geldings were the matched pair that pulled the carriage.

"The sorrel mare is Maria's," Ben mentioned. "She is an excellent rider. The blood-bay belongs to Manuel, but he seldom rides her any more. The draft horses pull the plows and other farm equipment."

Also grazing in the pasture were two milk cows and three head of cattle that would eventually be used for meat. Farther on, separated from the horses and cattle by a fence, were a dozen sheep and one ram. All of the animals appeared to be well-cared for.

They walked on to the fields where cotton had grown the previous year. There were ragged rows of dirt between the cotton stubble and weeds. William thought the earth looked pale. It was not the rich, black, Tennessee soil of his father's farm. He reached down and picked up a handful. Neither did it smell good; nor did it taste right.

Ben said the crop the last two or three years had been poor. There were fewer cotton bolls per plant, and there were four-or-five bales less than the years before.

Master Manuel had been very angry with Samuel and the slaves because production was so low. He was not a farmer. He didn't understand why production was less. He blamed Samuel and the slaves, calling them lazy. When Samuel tried to explain that the soil needed to rest and recover, Manuel hit him across the face with his riding crop. No one dared say anything else to Master Manuel.

Miss Olivia had been very upset with Manuel. She had told him he had no right to strike Samuel. He was a freeman.

Manuel had exploded at his mother for the rebuke. He stormed out of the house, ordered his horse, and rode into the city.

Ben finished his description of Manuel's reaction to the poor crop yield, and the trio left the worn out fields and walked back toward the house. Ben left them as they passed the barn. Jock and William walked on to the front of the house and sat down on the porch to wait for Miss Olivia.

William told Jock that the soil in the cotton fields had lost its growing power and needed to sit unused for at least one year, probably more. The fields should be planted with wild grasses. He explained his father had told him about fields like these in Virginia that would not grow anything but weeds. In Virginia they had started grazing horses and cattle in those fields. The droppings helped heal the soil. He didn't know exactly what was in the droppings, but the fields produced better after a year or two of resting and being grazed upon. His father rotated the fields on the farm using each field for a different purpose each year. This seemed to work because they always produced good crops.

Chapter Fourteen

Growing Confidence

They heard Miss Olivia calling to Sadie inside the house. In a few minutes, Miss Olivia came out the front door. William, followed by Jock, stood up as was proper manners when a lady entered. Fortunately, his father had taught his son some etiquette to be used around ladies.

"Well, did you get a look at the plantation?" Miss Olivia asked.

"Yes, we did," William answered. "You have some nice stock. The matched geldings for the carriage are beautiful. Your plantation is well-cared for."

"It doesn't produce crops like it did a few years ago when my husband was alive. My son thinks that my overseer is lazy and that the slaves should be beaten. It is their fault the cotton doesn't grow the way it once did."

"Then," she sadly added, "the slaves should be sold and new, younger, more energetic slaves purchased to grow the cotton. Manuel thinks Samuel should be dismissed and a white overseer hired."

"What do you think, William?" she asked. "You're a farmer."

William told Miss Olivia what he had previously said to Jock. He, also, suggested that another cash crop should be found to grow on some of the tired fields. Maybe hay or beans, he wasn't sure about crops in Louisiana. The right crop choice would take some investigating.

Miss Olivia seemed lost in thought when William finished. He did not interrupt her and sat patiently waiting.

Finally, turning to Jock, she requested, "Come over here next to me and tell me your story. I'm sure it is a fascinating one. You have had at least one fight," referring to the scar on his cheek, "which I'm sure you won based on your size and agility. And by your slight accent you are British not American. But I notice some salt in your language, which probably means you were a sailor at one time, in spite of your frontier clothes," she observed.

Very slowly, taking his time to pronounce each word, Jock replied, "You have a keen ear, and an observant eye, Miss Olivia. I grew up in London until I was twelve years old. At that impressionable age I went to sea aboard a British merchantman, and I have served on several ships since then. After a promotion I began to understand that to better my lot in life, I needed to learn as much as I could about my job and the jobs of the men around me and over me. But, more important, I learned that men respect other men who speak properly. I had thoughts of becoming a ship's officer, so I began to work on choosing the right words and getting rid of my heavy accent."

"When I was captured by Jean Lafitte's pirates and pressed into his service, I quickly discovered that remaining an ordinary seaman in his Navy might be the best place for me. I let my speech slip back to sound like the pirates I served with."

"Because General Jackson gave me a pardon and William and James became my friends, I have begun to try to improve my way of talking again, but when I get excited, angry, or frustrated, sometimes I forget, and my cockney words slip back into my language."

William had listened to Jock's reply to Miss Olivia's question very carefully. The Cockney accent and the rough-and-tumble language of the pirate had almost disappeared. This was not the first time he had noticed the big man controlling the words coming out of his mouth. Now, he knew why.

Jock told her of growing up in London and of his father's death. He also told her of his father's debt. He described his narrow escape, and how his mother had arranged to get him on the *Weavertree* as a Cabin Boy. Several years later, when he returned to London, he tried to find his mother only to learn she had died in debtor's prison.

Despite his mother's death, he knew he should repay his father's creditor. This he did. But the shylock claimed more was owed in interest. Jock had refused to pay the additional amount and left the man's establishment. The shylock, not being satisfied, came after him with two thugs. Jock being big for his age had fought for his life. In the fight that ensued, Jock killed the shylock and badly injured one of the thugs. However, the shylock, using pointed, iron knuckles, had cut Jock's cheek giving him the scar on his face.

The second thug had run to the police with a story of Jock refusing to pay money owed and picking a fight with poor innocent men.

Hurt and bleeding, Jock had made it back to his ship. The Captain did his best to sew up the cut. Fearing the authorities might come for Jock, the Captain had found a good hiding place for the wounded boy.

When the Crown Officers came looking for Jock, the Captain had told them that Jock had not returned, and if they didn't believe him, they could search the ship. The

Officers looked around the ship and not finding Jock, left. Jock remained hidden while the crew continued loading the cargo.

The next day the Officers returned saying Jock was wanted for assault and murder. This time they did a thorough search of the ship, but again did not find Jock who stayed well-hidden in the forward sail locker.

The Captain, thinking the authorities would return and demand his ship be held in port until Jock could be found, ordered the cargo loading finished and sailed on the evening tide.

Jock told of the pirate attack and becoming Jean Lafitte's ships' carpenter and of receiving a pardon from General Jackson to fight on the American side.

During the battle William had saved his life, and they had become good friends. With his pirate days pardoned and nothing but prison waiting for him in London, he had decided to stay in America. William had invited him to go to Tennessee to meet his family and to begin doing carpentry work in Russellville.

After seeing Maria on the balcony and knowing William's desire to return to New Orleans to find her, he decided to stay with his friend and search for the woman William cared so much about. That was how he got here. At this point in his story, Jock stopped talking.

Miss Olivia was looking at him intently.

"You are an honest young man," she remarked. "That is very refreshing. I can tell you did not hold anything back. Thank you, Jock, for telling me your story. Now, I know you both much better, and I feel more comfortable. I am not surprised that my daughter liked you and was willing to brave the wrath of my son and her fiancé."

She paused, thinking, then continued, "First, let me tell you about Fernando Hernandez, Maria's *so-called* Fiancé. He is smart, a good business man and has been very successful in several enterprises. But, he has a dark side; he is a gambler and a duelist. He is excellent with pistol, sword, rapier, knife, or fists. He likes to fight and has fought eleven duels winning them all. He was wounded in his last duel by a stray shot from his opponent. It seems that as the poor victim fell forward mortally wounded, his pistol went off, and the ball hit Fernando in the crotch. The story goes that part of his manhood was shot off, and he almost bled to death. Now, he can no longer have children. Maria does not know this."

"Although," she added thoughtfully, "since he was wounded, there has been some mellowing of his temper and disposition."

"However, Fernando's wound has not slowed his gambling, and he has won a lot of money at cards. He is not handsome, but not ugly either, well-to-do, powerful politically, possessive, and very jealous. He might kill anyone who threatened his possession of Maria."

Miss Olivia's last few words, William filed in his memory as something to remember when he would meet Fernando.

"Fernando has had dealings with Jean Lafitte in the slave market. Lafitte captures slave ships and brings the cargo to Barataria to resell to planters and dealers. Fernando buys some of the slaves, and then takes them North to rural areas of Louisiana and Mississippi to resell them for a large profit."

"Jock, do you know of those dealings?" Miss Olivia asked.

Jock replied that he had never been on one of Lafitte's ships that had captured a slave ship. He had been in Barataria once when a slave ship was brought in and had seen the slaves unloaded. They were a poor-looking group of people, skinny and dirty. The sight turned his stomach. The stench of the slave ship was all over the island. He and his shipmates were very happy to sail away on a patrol and to get some fresh air. One of his shipmates told him the slaves would be sold. The slaves and the slave ship were gone when his ship returned to Barataria. That was all he knew.

"I'm glad you had no dealings with the slaves," Miss Olivia commented.

She changed the subject to Maria, explaining that she knew of Maria's dancing in taverns for tips. That Ben and Sarah and sometimes Aunt Elizabeth, although Elizabeth didn't really approve, helped Maria with her disguises as a peasant girl. Ben and Sarah drove her to the back of the tavern in the enclosed carriage. Maria would change clothes in the carriage. Her excuse for these dancing forays was shopping for new clothes and then returning to be fitted. Neither Manuel nor Fernando had any desire to go dress shopping with Maria.

"Maria told me about you, William, and the afternoon you spent with her in the park. She really likes you, and she was looking forward to dancing for you again. But she was afraid for you because if Manuel found out about her seeing you, he might try to harm you. That was the reason she didn't want to know your name or you to know hers for your protection and hers. If she were found out, neither Manuel nor Fernando would know whom to look for." She paused, thinking.

"Maria wanted to see you again, but sadly, Manuel learned of her dancing and about you."

"Manuel threatened to tell Fernando about Maria's dancing and her friendship with you, but thought better of the idea because he might lose Fernando as a brother-in-law and business partner."

"Ben learned of your search for Maria from a servant in one of the taverns where Maria danced. Maria sent Ben and Sarah to warn you of the danger and to break off any further contact. You were in too much danger from Manuel. She believed that Manuel would hire some men to do you harm. You must be very careful." Miss Olivia warned.

"Do you think one of those men might be Ortega?" William asked.

"I don't know," Miss Olivia replied. "But, whoever the men might be, they wouldn't know your name or your militia company. However, William, when you had shouted at Maria and Manuel had realized that you were Maria's secret friend, I thought Manuel might send his men to talk to your company and learn about you."

William shifted uneasily. This realization unnerved him. William saw that Jock did not like it either.

Miss Olivia cautioned, "Manuel had confronted Maria about the man who had yelled at her. Her answer had been that some soldier thought she looked nice. She had no idea who it was in that bunch of marching men. Fernando had accepted her explanation not knowing of your meeting. Manuel had not."

"Fernando won a mercantile business in St. Louis not long ago," continued Miss Olivia. "He planned to travel there to take possession and dispose of it. Manuel manipulated Fernando into taking Maria, Aunt Elizabeth, and him along. Manuel reasoned that the trip would bring Fernando and Maria closer. The trip would also get Maria away from New Orleans and William. Maria did not want to go, but Manuel had said Fernando might withdraw his support of the family business if she did not go. They started yesterday on that new steamboat."

"I had tried to keep Maria in New Orleans, but Manual shouted me down and told me not to interfere. He told me that if I interfered, he would throw me out on the street, broke. Because my solicitor had advised me not to confront Manuel until he had completed some legal work to cement my ownership of the plantation, the city house, and other properties, I let Manuel have his way for the moment," Miss Olivia went on.

"My son is not a nice man, and someday he will be unable to lie, cheat, steal, or buy his way out of trouble," admitted Miss Olivia. "Manuel thinks he knows everything, but he does not know much about the law and inheritance," she sighed. "My solicitor is helping me protect all of my property for Maria. The family trading business will be Manuel's only inheritance."

"Now that you know the trouble Maria's in, do you still want to help her? Please do not answer me now," she motioned with her hand as William started to reply. "I want you to think seriously about what you will be taking on. You will need to go to St. Louis, extricate Maria from Señor Hernandez and Manual, and return her to me," she finished and quietly looked down at her hands in her lap.

William studied Miss Olivia. For the first time since they had met, the tension in her face seemed to melt away.

"It will be dark soon and we will have dinner. Will you stay the night here with me? There are two bedrooms available for your use upstairs." Miss Olivia's gentle smile and her relaxed body language welcomed the two men into her home.

William and Jock readily accepted.

Chapter Fifteen

The Promise

William sat on the porch in the growing dusk deep in thought; Jock had gone to the barn to get their gear, and Miss Olivia was inside to see about dinner. This situation had become a much more complicated one than he could ever have imagined. What had he gotten them into?

Jock returned with their rifles and blankets. He sat down next to William, and shared, "Blue Belle says she misses us, but she's happy in her stall with fresh hay, and Ben indicated he knew we would be staying the night. He will see us in the morning."

William nodded his assent but said nothing. *He was being hunted, probably by a man named Ortega whom he had seen very briefly at the tavern. Could he recognize that man if he saw him again? He wasn't sure. Jock had had a better look at Ortega.*

William asked Jock, "Would you recognize Ortega if you saw him again?"

"I think so," Jock replied, hesitantly.

"Whatever you decide to do is fine with me. I'm with you no matter what happens," Jock emphasized.

"Thank you."

Jock is a true friend, William thought, *as he mulled over the problems. A plan began to form in his mind.*

Just then, Sadie called the two men to dinner. The meal was delicious. The conversation continued on the plantation and William's ideas about the crops and the planting. Miss Olivia had decided to put William's idea into action about the pasture and moving the animals to the old used up cotton fields. Of course, a fence needed be built to keep the animals in, but her people could do this with the current supply of fence posts and by felling some trees in the nearby woods.

William had another idea for Miss Olivia. The two mares could be bred if there was a stud on one of the nearby plantations. She might need to give the stud owner one of the foals as payment for the breeding, for example, one foal for four successful breedings. This idea about the breeding would increase her herd and produce another area for income. Miss Olivia liked the idea, too.

After dinner Miss Olivia excused herself saying, she had some things to do in her room. She said she was tired from the last two days' stress and needed some rest. After pointing out the two bedrooms for the men and two lamps for them to use, she retired to her room, closing the door behind her.

William and Jock went out on the porch to sit and talk. They were not yet ready for sleep.

Sitting in the dark with only the thin candlelight that filtered through the door and windows, William reviewed his thinking with Jock.

"Manuel's men have probably caught up with the company by now and know our names and descriptions. If we follow the road the company took, Manuel's men will probably be waiting for us. But if we are dressed as something other than militia men and driving a horse and cart, they would first have to make sure they had found the right men. That would give us a leg-up. Then, we can discourage them from looking any further."

"I think I can fix the cart so that we can carry our rifles in side scabbards ready to use in a moment's notice," Jock said.

The two men fell silent. Each with his own thoughts. The air grew cooler. A couple of shivers and they went in and up to bed. William lay awake for a long time thinking. *Accepting Miss Olivia's request would be a big challenge and responsibility. Certainly, Maria was well worth it.*

William awoke to voices from below. He stretched and rubbed his eyes. After spending the last five months sleeping on the ground, sleeping in a bed with sheets had given him a real, deep sleep. He felt energized and dressed quickly. When he reached the first floor, Jock and Miss Olivia were already sitting at the table. Sadie brought in a large platter of eggs and ham slices. They used fresh bread to clean their plates. The men had good appetites, and the food was quickly gone. Miss Olivia said she liked men with good appetites.

After eating, the three went into the parlor. William and Jock took seats near Miss Olivia's chair.

"Well, William, what have you decided?" Miss Olivia asked. "Jock, I know will go with you whatever you decide."

"I care for Maria very much. Her happiness is important to me. I will go to St Louis and find Maria, and I will help her out of this entrapment. I will try to convince Manuel that Maria is her own woman and must be allowed to do what she wishes to do. And, I will free her from Señor Hernandez," William said.

"William, are you familiar with the Spanish custom of young ladies' families arranging marriages for their daughters?" Miss Olivia asked. "I did not hold to it when I was a young girl, and I do not hold with it now. My family did not try to force a marriage on me. They knew I would not agree. I had a mind of my own and would follow my own way. My family was smart. Manuel, on the other hand, is not smart. He believes, because he is a man and the only male in the family, he can make decisions for Maria and me."

"Well, he can't." Miss Olivia stated emphatically. "Maria has a mind of her own, and she should follow her dreams."

"There is something else you need to know." Miss Olivia continued, "I believe Manuel has something he is holding over Fernando's head to force him to do whatever Manuel wishes--something in addition to Maria's hand. I do not know what it is."

"Maria loves her brother," Miss Olivia went on. "She believes she is helping her brother save the family business by sacrificing herself to help him. You, William, must convince her that her brother really does not love her and that he just wants to dominate her and secure Fernando's continual supply of money. You must tell her to follow her dreams not Manuel's. Now, I come to the hard part for you, William. If you set Maria free, she may not want to stay with you on a farm. She may want to go to Spain to study dance," Miss Olivia confessed.

At this statement William felt a pain in his heart. *This thought had occurred to him, but it being said out loud hurt. Why would Maria not want what he wanted. He did not like this thought. He loved Maria and she loved him. Why would she not want to spend the rest of her life with him?*

Miss Olivia watched him closely. So did Jock. They could see the conflict in his face. They waited. *Well, the only way he would know was to set Maria free, and then ask her to marry him. He could be very persuasive when he needed to be. He was quite sure he could persuade her to say, "yes" and marry him.*

"Thank you for the warning, but I will let Maria decide her future." William stated flatly.

"I knew you would say that," said Miss Olivia resolutely. "I want a promise from each of you to return Maria to me."

William and Jock gave their word.

With that she pulled four envelopes from her pocket.

"This first letter," she announced, handing it to William, "is to my son Manuel. It states my disapproval of this arranged marriage to Fernando Hernandez. And that any marriage for Maria must have my consent. If Manuel persists, then he will be cut off from the family business, the city house, and the plantation. There will be no income from me or my estate. He will be on his own. The law is on my side as the courts of New Orleans have decreed. I received the papers too late to prevent Maria's leaving for St Louis."

"This second letter is to my daughter. I am telling her that she is free to follow her heart. She does not need to marry Fernando. She does not need to do as Manuel says. I am setting up an endowment for her which will provide her with an income for the rest of her life. Manuel cannot get his hands on this money," she smiled slightly when the words were out of her mouth.

"This third letter is to Fernando Hernandez, informing him that Manuel's promise of Maria's hand in marriage is cancelled by her family and that Maria is free to make up her own mind about whom she wishes to marry."

"This fourth letter contains instructions for my solicitor. This letter includes a change to my will. It will introduce you and Jock as friends and ask him to help you with your search for Maria." Miss Olivia took out a bag of coins. "There is $1,250 in silver and gold in this bag. To my solicitor for his services, $50 is to be given. The rest is for your expenses and to be used for Maria's return to

New Orleans. I plan to be here when she returns, but my health is not good, and the doctors have told me my time is limited."

William answered with conviction. "I will do everything in my power to fulfill your requests." *He hoped he could do all he promised.*

"I know you will, William. You and Jock have my complete trust. Ben will return to the city with you and show you where my solicitor's office is located. You can return Ben to the city house. Thank you for coming to see me. You're both good men. Maria is lucky to have friends like you. I hope I can count you as my friends, also."

"You can," William said and Jock nodded his agreement.

"We need to return to the militia company so that I'm not listed as a deserter. If those men Manuel hired are looking for me, then they will be on the road waiting. Trouble is best faced head on. I don't want to be looking over my shoulder, wondering when someone will shoot me from ambush. Manuel's men will not expect us in a horse drawn cart. If we are dressed in old farm clothes we might fool them. Do you have any old clothes we could use as a disguise?" William asked.

"There are some old work clothes that belonged to my husband that might fit you, William. Jock is so big that Sadie and I may need to make a large shirt that will cover a sizable portion of his buckskin pants," replied Miss Olivia.

When they were ready to leave, Miss Olivia walked out onto the porch with them. Blue Belle and Ben were waiting at the hitching post. The cart was loaded with their rifles and blankets. A bag of food had also been included. Jock's slings for their rifles hung in easy reach on both sides of the seat.

She gave a brief hug to both men. "Goodbye and God go with you," she said solemnly.

The men climbed onto the cart, and said goodbye. William started Blue Belle down the path to the road and New Orleans. They turned and waved before disappearing behind the trees that lined the road. Miss Olivia was still standing on the porch, waving. Sadie stood beside her. Samuel leaned against the hitching post.

Chapter Sixteen

Road to Baton Rouge

Miss Olivia's solicitor's office was only a few blocks from her city house. While William and Jock entered the office building, Ben stayed with Blue Belle and the sulky.

The solicitor's office was on the second floor behind a big, polished, wooden door. The solicitor's name, painted in large block letters, was on the door. Attorney at Law was underneath. The reception room contained four small desks. Two of the desks were occupied by young men. On opposite walls were shelves of books. A large portrait of a stern-looking man dominated the wall behind the two men. Two uncomfortable-looking, wooden chairs sat facing the occupied desks.

An older gentleman, sitting behind the desk labeled "Secretary" looked up and offered his assistance as William and Jock entered.

William stated his business to the secretary, who disappeared through a door marked "Private." Almost immediately the secretary returned and ushered them into the solicitor's office. A man of fifty-or-more-years in a black coat rose from behind the desk and shook hands with both men. He was of average height and weight with thinning salt and pepper hair and spectacles. His eyes conveyed intelligence. Motioning them to chairs on the opposite side of his big desk, he returned to his seat.

"How may I help you, young men," he inquired.

William produced Miss Olivia's letter and the fifty dollars. Two hours later they concluded their business and returned to the street.

Ben guided them back to the city house. Sarah came out of the back door as they drove up to the barn. She said, "Hello" and looked unspoken questions at Ben.

Ben climbed down and said, "Goodbye." Excitedly, he told Sarah he would tell her everything and that William and Jock were going to help Maria and Miss Olivia. William turned Blue Belle around and started the long ride to Baton Rouge and their militia company.

When they were out of town and away from prying eyes, William stopped the sulky. Quickly, they changed into the old clothes that Miss Olivia had provided, checked the loads in their guns, and made some adjustments to the rifle scabbards for quicker access. They would be ready if Manuel's hired men showed up.

William asked Jock if he would like to drive. He said he would, so William gave him the reins. Jock learned fast. Blue Belle seemed to know Jock was driving and was very cooperative.

As the sun slid below the treetops, they began looking for a place to camp for the night. William suggested that they get as far back in the woods and away from the road as they could and not light a fire. It didn't take them long to find an opening in the trees large enough to drive away from the road. William hopped from the seat as Blue Belle pulled the sulky into the woods. With a leafy branch, he brushed away their tracks. Next, he pulled branches and some brush into the space where the sulky had entered. Standing in the middle of the road, he surveyed his work. Only an experienced tracker would be able to spot where they turned off. The men hunting him were probably city bred and not skilled at reading signs.

Using the leafy branch, he brushed away his footprints and entered the woods some distance from the sulky's entry point.

Blue Belle had taken Jock to a grassy depression beside a small brook. They were well away from the road. The shallow flow of water made soft gurgles over and around the exposed rocks, muffling the sounds of their presence.

Jock had Blue Belle unhitched and enjoying a well-deserved drink when William caught up with them. Blue Belle stood with her two front feet in the water, lapping as fast as she could. When she wanted no more, Jock led her to the largest patch of grass to graze.

William moved the sulky into a blocking position just below the edge of the depression. He cut some branches and laid them over the sulky. Anyone approaching from the road would not see it. Satisfied, he moved into the campsite.

Jock had their blanket rolls spread on the grass and the food bag open. They ate a cold meal then found comfortable sleeping positions on their blankets. They were tired. The sounds of the horse's munching on grass and the brook's gurgles lulled them to sleep.

William awoke suddenly. Had he heard something not right? He lay perfectly still, eyes open, and listened to the sounds of the forest. The horse shifted a hoof but was not chewing grass. Slowly, he focused his eyes to look at her. Blue Belle had her head up with ears pointed forward. She was looking toward the road. The soft clop, clop of horse's hooves hitting the ground came to him. He looked toward Jock who was also awake. A low murmur of voices floated through the trees.

William motioned for Jock to stay with the horse so she would not give away their position. He moved away from the camp staying parallel to the road, then angled forward. Soundlessly, he moved through trees and brush. As he approached the road, he could see two men on horseback silhouetted in the moonlight filtering through the canopy. They were talking in the soft tones people often used at night. Their horses walked slowly up the road unaware of Blue Belle being nearby.

The riders were neither in a hurry nor were they searching for signs of other travelers. William could see the men but not their faces. One was smaller than the other. Ortega and Chavez, maybe? He couldn't be sure, or they might just be late travelers. He listened, but only two words were distinguishable from their conversation, "Baton Rouge."

The men and horses disappeared around a curve in the road. William remained where he crouched, listening. He heard nothing unusual, just the night sounds of the forest.

When he returned to camp, Jock was waiting, his rifle ready. He stood beside Blue Belle whose jaws were turning grass into an easily, digestible mulch. She looked up as he neared the camp, then recognizing William, she put her head down for another mouthful. William quickly explained to Jock what he had seen and heard.

"I don't believe they were looking for us," he said under his breath, "but maybe we should keep a watch for the rest of the night."

"I take the first watch," Jock offered, sitting down with his back to a tree.

The night was cold. William lay down and snuggled into his blankets. Their warmth quickly put him to sleep. It was still dark when Jock woke him for his watch. Jock lay down and went to sleep almost at once. William got up and walked around the camp. Blue Belle stood quiet, sleeping. Two hours or more of night remained before dawn. William did not know the time when the travelers had passed. It had been about midnight, he judged. Listening and waiting, his watch passed quickly and quietly.

An hour after dawn found them several miles from where they had camped. They were following the hoof prints of the horses that had passed in the night. Eventually, the hoof prints turned off onto a wagon path, leading away from the road. William climbed from the sulky and jogged down the path, following its curve out of sight deeper into the forest. There had been no hurry in the horses and riders. Satisfied there was no hidden danger, he returned to Jock and Blue Belle. They continued on toward Baton Rouge.

The road took a long, slow curve to the west. Blue Belle was setting a good pace. William figured they would reach Baton Rouge by late afternoon if they continued at this speed. They passed a small plantation. The road turned north for a mile or two then curved eastward. It seemed to be following the "S" curves of the Mississippi River.

As they came to a straight stretch in the road that extended for maybe a quarter of a mile, William began to get an uneasy feeling. If they were going to be confronted by Manuel's men, it would need to be soon. Baton Rouge was only a few miles ahead. Jock had the same idea. They checked their weapons and slowed Blue Belle to a walk. They did not want to drive into an ambush at top speed.

Jock stopped the sulky. They sat and listened. Both men could sense something was not right. Blue Belle was looking down the road. She heard other horses and whinnied. Down the road and to one side came an answering whinny. William pulled his rifle from its scabbard. He heard Jock cock his pistol under his big, loose-fitting shirt.

121

Two men on horseback rode out from a wagon path at the side of the road and faced them. William felt sure they were the men who had passed during the night. *How had these men gotten so far ahead when they had turned off only a few miles beyond our camp?* William thought. *That path must have been a short cut to here. Now was not the time to ask those questions.*

A sinister grin filled the thin, hawk-like face of the smaller man. In his hand was a saddle pistol. The other man had a gloomy look. He adjusted the musket that rested across his saddle.

"That's the man from the tavern," Jock whispered. "The big one must be Chavez."

The men walked their horses toward the sulky. Their weapons were ready but not pointed at Jock or William. After all, William was holding his rifle. They did not know Jock was armed because Jock's rifle was in its scabbard next to him.

"Your horse spoiled our little surprise, Señor Russell . . Señor Smith," the thin man, said, referring to the Blue Belle's whinny. The men drew within pistol range and stopped.

"Oh yes, we know your names," he said, responding to the silence that met their greeting. "Your militia company helped with that information. We even know your company commander's name. We caught up with your company and learned a great deal about you."

The glum looking man joined in, "We learned the most about you from the old man and his woman. Of course, we had to beat it out of them, but that was fun," the man said sadistically. "That old man was tough for a slave. He took a lot of punishment before he gave you up. The old woman wouldn't tell us much. But then, she couldn't stand the beating the old man was taking, so she told us all she knew."

"You beat up Ben and Sarah to learn about us? . . .

You sadistic bastards," William exploded, a cold furry in his voice. "They didn't know anything!"

"Oh, but they did. They knew that you were driving a horse cart, that you had left for Baton Rouge yesterday, and that you had learned Señorita Maria had left New Orleans. The old man told us everything before he died," sneered the man facing William.

"Ortega, you and Chavez are going to pay dearly," William stated emphatically.

The use of their names caught them by surprise. It gave William and Jock the edge they needed.

"NOW!" William dove off the sulky, hitting the ground and rolling toward the side of the road. Ortega's pistol exploded, and the ball imbedded itself into the dirt where William had landed. At the sudden gunshot, Ortega's horse reared and tried to turn and run. William had rolled onto his back bringing his rifle up. He fired at Ortega. Blood blossomed from Ortega's neck.

Jock had fired his pistol as William jumped. Chavez's musket never reached an aiming point. The ball from Jock's pistol hit Chavez in the chest, knocking him backward from his horse. His musket went off as he fell. The shot kicked up the dirt in front of Blue Belle causing her to jump. Chavez was dead when he hit the ground.

Ortega quieted his horse, and then put his hand to his neck. Blood ran out between his fingers. His pistol lay in the dust of the road where he had dropped it. There was no more fight in the man. The musket in the scabbard under his leg remained in its place.

Jock reloaded his pistol and pointed it at Ortega. William had quickly regained his footing, reloading as he did.

"You shot me. I'm bleeding to death," Ortega cried, leveling a string of curses at his captors.

"Señor Manuel Olivarez will kill you for what you have done. He is a very important man in New Orleans."

More curses followed.

"Get down from your horse, and we'll take a look at the wound," Jock said. Ortega got down still holding his neck. While William kept his rifle aimed at Ortega's chest, Jock walked over to him, checked him for other weapons, and removed a knife from his boot.

"Now, let me see your neck," Jock said, pulling the bloody fingers away. "That's a flesh wound. The ball missed your artery, so you won't bleed to death, although it might be better for you if you did. Killing old Ben will get you hung."

"They were slaves. You don't get hung for killing slaves," Ortega sneered.

"You killed Sarah, too?" Jock asked angrily.

"She died after we hit her a couple of times," Ortega responded.

"You'll get hung for killing them. They weren't slaves, but free," William furiously replied.

"Señor Olivarez said they were his slaves," the man argued.

"Señor Olivarez isn't very smart. There is a lot he doesn't know, and when I find him, he'll learn how dumb he really is," William replied, still very angry.

Jock had walked to Ortega's horse and opened his saddle bag. He took out a dirty shirt and threw it at him. "Wrap that around your neck."

"You're going looking for big trouble if you try to find Señor Olivarez because Señor Fernando Hernandez is with him," Ortega said, not backing down. "Those two will not hesitate to kill you both."

"We will find them, and they will wish we hadn't! Never fear," William retorted, as he pulled a rope from Ortega's saddle.

They tied Ortega's hands then draped him over the saddle of his horse after removing the musket and checking for hidden weapons. They folded Chavez over his saddle, also. The horses with their human cargo were tied to the back of the sulky.

William and Jock's entrance into Baton Rouge caused a stir of excitement. People began following them toward the Marshal's Office.

The Marshal, his badge clearly visible on his chest, stood in front of his office watching them approach. He had an intelligent, no nonsense appearance. He was tall with a wiry look and clear, piercing, blue eyes. He said nothing, waiting for an explanation. Standing behind the marshal was a deputy.

"William . . . Jock," James shouted and waved from across the street. "I'll bet you have some story to tell." He walked across the street, followed by Sam and Matt. He glanced at the two men slung over their saddles, "Say, those are the two men who were hanging around our camp looking for you and asking a lot of questions about you, William."

Jock brought Blue Belle to a stop in front of the Marshal.

Ortega let out a curse and grumbled he was being held against his will. He was innocent and should be untied.

"Marshal, these men tried to kill us a few miles back," William explained before dismounting from the sulky. "We defended ourselves and they lost. A man named Manuel Olivarez hired them to kill us. These men also killed an old man and old woman in New Orleans trying to get information on us."

"Get that man down and bring him inside," the Marshal instructed his deputy, indicating Ortega. "You two men come into my office and you three men, too," pointing at James, Sam, and Matt. "Billy, you go get the Coroner for the dead man." A young man, standing nearby turned and ran down the street.

The Marshal turned on his heel and entered his office

going to a desk in the corner; the deputy followed with the cursing Ortega in tow. William, Jock, James, Sam, and Matt joined the Marshal facing the desk.

The office was sparsely equipped. The desk, a desk chair, and three other chairs completed the furnishings. A gun rack hung on the wall with several muskets and pistols under a chain lock. The jail cells were through a thick wooden door at the rear of the room. The Marshal indicated that Ortega was to be put into one of the cells. Then, he sat down at his desk, got out some paper, dipped his quill in the inkwell, and said, "Tell me what happened. You first," indicating William.

William and Jock described the events leading up to the fight with the two men. Then, they described the encounter and fight in detail. The Marshal wrote while they talked. He continued writing for a few moments after they completed their story.

"Please read this," the Marshal said, "and if it is correct, sign it." He handed the paper to William who read it to Jock. William signed the paper and Jock made his mark.

The Marshal turned to James, Sam, and Matt who had been patiently waiting. "Tell me your involvement with these men."

James stepped forward, explaining that William and Jock were in their militia company. The prisoner and the dead man had come into their camp the night they left New Orleans, asking a lot of questions about the man who had yelled at the girl on the balcony. They were trying to learn his name and where he was. James and the other militia men did not like the questioning, and Captain Stewart ordered the men out of camp. Whether the men learned about William and Jock, he did not know.

The Marshal handed James another paper to read and sign. James read and signed the paper as did Sam and Matt.

The door to the office opened, and Captain Stewart came in. He introduced himself to the Marshal. A quick explanation and the Captain agreed with James' accounting of the two men he had ordered out of camp. He added that the men left without an argument, so he believed that they had learned the names of William and Jock, and that they had returned to New Orleans.

Captain Stewart said, "My company must leave tomorrow. I'd like to take my men with me."

The Marshal said that James, Sam, and Matt could go, but Jock and William must stay in Baton Rouge to testify before the judge who would be arriving in a week. William and Jock would be free as long as they stayed in town.

Captain Stewart gave both William and Jock papers granting them permission to stay in Baton Rouge as long as the Marshal needed them. They were then to catch up with the company. James also decided to stay.

The next morning the company marched out of town headed for Tennessee. Watching them go were William, James, Jock and Blue Belle.

Chapter Seventeen

Baton Rouge

Baton Rouge, a small town of a thousand souls didn't offer much for a soldier to do. William and his friends were going to be there for a week or more waiting for the Ortega trial.

"What are we going to do until the trial?" James asked.

"I have an idea. We can get some jobs doing carpentry work," Jock suggested.

"You can help me. I have my tools." Jock had returned to Barataria before leaving New Orleans to get some personal things and his tools. He had retrieved the tools from one of the wagons before the company continued their march.

"That sounds like a good idea," William replied.

During the week Jock, James, and William did several jobs for the merchants and the people of Baton Rouge. Jock shared the fees with William and James. By the start of the trial, each had earned more than a month's Army pay.

At the trial, the Marshal told them that his deputy had

returned from New Orleans with the news that Ben and Sarah had been found by the authorities. Señora Olivia Olivarez had taken care of their burial. The New Orleans' authorities had witnesses to the beatings and knew the identities of the men who had committed the crimes. Both men had a history of trouble with the law. After the trial in Baton Rouge, Ortega would be sent to New Orleans for trial on the murders of Ben and Sarah.

The Marshal, also, had gotten Ortega to confess about Manuel Olivarez's hiring him to hunt down William and to kill him and anybody else who had known or seen Maria dance. The Marshal issued a warrant for Manuel Olivarez's arrest for conspiracy to commit murder and for murder.

Ortega's trial took all of two hours. The jury found him guilty of attempted murder, and the judge sentenced him to twenty years imprisonment for the crime.

Early the next morning, William, James, and Jock loaded the cart, hitched up Blue Belle, and set out to find their militia company.

Four days later in the late afternoon, the three men caught up with the company. The supply wagons were at the rear of the column. They slowed Blue Belle to a walk as she approached the last wagon.

"Let's see how long we can follow without being seen," Jock said and the other two grinned in agreement.

When the men in the company realized that William, James, and Jock were following the last wagon, they burst out laughing.

"How long you boys been there?" They asked."

"Almost an hour," Jock told them.

The men were surprised. Everyone enjoyed the joke. The trio were happy to be back with their company.

Chapter Eighteen

Lone Bear

The men's spirits were high even though it was a long and tiring walk home. William thought much about Maria Olivarez. *He began to plan his trip to St. Louis and how he would conduct their reunion. First, he needed to go home so that his parents would know he had survived the war. Also, he needed to introduce Jock to his family and help him get his carpentry work started. Finally, he needed to help his father get the spring planting finished.*

James' shoulder had healed nicely; however, he still had a lot of weakness in his right hand. James exercised it as much as he could to get his strength back.

Captain Stewart knew James and William had lived on the frontier all of their lives and were known to be good hunters. So after several days on the march, he sent them out to find some game to supplement their meager stores of rice, beans, dried beef, and pemmican.

Jock accompanied William and James on their hunting trips. He wanted to learn how to quietly approach game and how to skin and to cure hides. Sam and Matt agreed to drive Blue Belle while Jock was hunting. Jock proved to be a surprisingly quiet walker through the leaves and brush. He had traded with one of the militiamen for some moccasins.

The hunters would start off by jogging down the road in front of the company for about a mile. They needed to get away from the sounds of the marching men. Too much noise would scare the game away. Whoever was in the lead would look for a game trail that ran away from the road. If the trail looked used, he would follow it slowing the pace some. The other two men would bring up the rear.

On this day, James--who led the trio--selected a game trail that had seen recent activity. James saw several leaves that had been turned over by the passing of some animal. The turned-over leaves were dry on the up side-- not wet from the previous night's rain. Cautiously, they moved forward.

The trail led to a large open field where the trees that had lived there had been broken and knocked over by some long-passed storm. Long, green grass and weeds had grown up around those dead trees and stumps. The dark gray of the decaying matter contrasted with the vibrant greens of the new growth. Some of the trees had broken high up and now stood like sentinels with a few, knarled, leafless branches that looked like deformed arms. A large, red-tailed hawk sat on one of those branches searching the grass for a meal. Suddenly, it left its perch and dove into the grass out of sight, emerging again after a moment with a mouse clutched tightly in its talons. It flew off toward the forest.

"There goes a mother to feed her young," James commented.

Shortly after noon they shot two turkeys feeding in the grass. The company really enjoyed their evening meal that night. They gobbled up their food eagerly. The lip-smacking, happy chatter while chewing, and some finger licking could be heard all over the camp.

When the company left New Orleans, it had been given orders to improve the roads as they marched north. They were now in the northern part of the Mississippi Territory, and the road had become little more than a trail. Several times a day the company had to stop and make the road wide enough for the wagons to pass. More than once fallen trees had to be cleared from their path.

One narrow river crossing required a small bridge to be built. The men didn't mind the work because other future travelers would benefit from an improved road. The country was growing, and better roads would be needed to move products and goods to market.

When it rained, the going became very slow because the road turned to mud. The temperature always dropped when it rained. The farther north they marched, the more likely the chance of freezing rain or snow. Rain-swollen streams were always dangerous when a safe crossing could not be found. Sometimes the men had to work for hours to build a crossing so the heavy wagons would not bog down. This extra work always brought the march to a snail's pace, and the men grumbled. They were ready to get back to good ol' Tennessee.

Every day it didn't rain, the trio went hunting, always looking for game trails that took them into the dense forest that surrounded the road. Sometimes, the hunters traveled several miles from the company's line of march to find game. For several days the hunting was without luck, and the men had to return empty handed. Captain Stewart decided to send out two different hunting parties, one to the east and another to the west. This new strategy helped considerably as one or the other group usually brought in some game.

One cold, crisp morning even in the sunshine, William led James and Jock silently through the trees along a promising game trail. William felt some anxiety because yesterday they had found no game. He judged that they were probably four miles from the company, so he knew there would be no noise to scare the game. Animals give themselves away by changing their position, so when William saw a movement ahead, he held up his hand for James and Jock to stop. There was a meadow opening up in front of him no bigger than an acre, and something was moving at its edge in the cover of the trees. A four-point buck gingerly stepped onto the meadow grass. After carefully looking around, it lowered its head and began to graze.

William crept forward to a large tree where he could clearly see the deer. Jock and James remained quiet and still where they had stopped. A noise or movement might startle the buck, and there would be no shot at all. William aimed and squeezed the trigger. The buck jumped high, turning from the impact of the ball and immediately disappeared into the brush. The sounds of it crashing forward could clearly be heard. William ran forward toward the place the buck had disappeared, reloading as he went. Into the brush William ran. Jock and James walked after him. They didn't need to hurry. William was already there.

About thirty feet into the trees, William found the deer. It had fallen in an open area with a deadfall and dense brush on two sides. The deer was dead. William set his rifle against a large tree with his powder horn, hunting belt, and pouch. Because he did not want to get his jacket stained while preparing the deer for transport, he removed it and hung it on a tree branch. The air was cold, but the sunlight coming through the branches felt warm. There were patches of snow in the shadows of the trees. He rolled up the sleeves of his shirt, pulled his knife, and knelt beside the deer to start the cleaning. There was a noise behind him. He didn't look back because he was sure James and Jock had followed him through the trees. Something slammed into the back of his head with a sickening thud. His lights went out as the ground came up to meet him.

William lay unconscious on the ground next to the deer. Four men stood looking down at him.

"That will fix you, you little cheater," Henry Schmitt exclaimed through a crooked grin.

James came through the brush behind them.

"What happened?" he demanded, seeing William unconscious on the ground. James held his rifle in the crook of his left arm with his right hand around the trigger guard.

He did not point his rifle at the men, but he was ready if they made a move.

The four men turned to face him.

"Hello, James. I might have known you would be trailing along behind William," Henry Schmitt sneered.

"He tried to steal our deer," growled one of the other men.

"William shot the deer," James said, fully aware that they were all looking at him with unfriendly eyes. James knew Henry Schmitt. He also recognized the man next to Henry from the confrontation on the street in New Orleans. The other two he did not know.

"No he didn't. I shot that buck," growled Henry's friend.

"What happened to him?" James said, pointing to William on the ground. He could see William's hunting knife in his hand and his rifle propped against a nearby tree.

"I hit him with the butt of my rifle when he tried to gut our deer," Henry Schmitt smirked.

William moved and let out a moan from the pain. He struggled to put his hand on the back of his head.

"Ohooo, what . . ." He tried unsuccessfully to move

again.

One of the unknown men taunted, "he taint hurt none."

"You like getting hit over the head with a gun-butt?" James asked.

The man looked at James and grinned an ugly grin. "You want to do something about it, you being alone?"

With that, a premonition swept over James that Jock was not behind him as he had first thought. Where was he? James dared not take his eyes off the men. William would be of no help. William groaned again and moved trying to sit up, but James could see that William was not fully conscious.

These men thought James and William were alone, so they had the advantage. They started to move toward James.

Henry began to raise his rifle to hit the prone William again. From behind him came a deep-throated growl as Jock burst from the brush, and in two, lighting-fast steps he came up beside Henry who turned too slowly toward the sound. A crushing, left fist slammed into Henry's head just behind his temple. Henry's legs buckled, his rifle fell from his hands, and he collided with the ground next to William. He lay motionless.

Jock stepped over Henry's body and brought a hard-driven, left backhand to the face of the man who claimed to have shot the deer, knocking him backward into the other two men who let him sit down hard on the ground.

In a voice with a heavy cockney accent, Jock said angrily, "So ye shot de deer?" He addressed the sitting man. "Pull de trigger of yer gun, so let's see."

The other two men turned a little and fidgeted uneasily. Someone, unseen, had come in behind them again. He had knocked Henry out with one blow, and now Henry's friend was sitting on the ground with a quickly, darkening left eye. His rifle lay across his legs out of easy reach. They had been unaware of this big man, and now he was pointing his gun at them, as was James.

"That won't prove anything. I reloaded," cried the man on the ground.

"Der has not been enough time to reload; besides I've been watching ye," answered Jock. "Pull de trigger or I'll pull it for ye."

"Now, wait a minute," the man protested.

"Pull the trigger," Jock demanded, his voice low and menacing as he stepped forward.

Jock's rifle was pointed at the sitting man. The other two stood still. William was conscious now and moved a little to sit up. The three men didn't notice; their attention was on the big man with the rifle. James' rifle now angled toward the nearest man. Jock moved closer to the sitting man who claimed to be the shooter. Without perception of movement, Jock jammed the muzzle of his weapon hard into the man's chest, causing him to fall backwards. As the man fell, Jock scooped up the rifle with his left hand. The man looked at Jock, grimacing from the blow. The other two men backed up a step.

"Stay steady," William said to the men. He had retrieved his rifle and now pointed it at them.

Jock pulled the trigger of the man's rifle which immediately exploded. The rifle ball went up through the trees overhead. He tossed the rifle to the side of the clearing.

"I told you I reloaded."

"Liar," was all Jock said.

"Pull the triggers on your guns and set them down over there with his rifle," James said. Seeing they didn't have much choice, the men complied.

Jock picked up Henry's weapon and discharged it and put it with the others. Then, he instructed the men to pick Henry up and put him near the fallen tree on the other side of the clearing from William. After complying with Jock's instructions, the men sat down around Henry's unconscious body.

James noticed one of the two men had a British Bearskin hat partly sticking out of his pack.

"What regiment were you with at New Orleans?" he asked.

The men looked at him curious like. How did he know?

"I saw the Bearskin," James said.

The men explained that they had been with the Kentucky militia. Their small group had been with Colonel Coffee for over a year and had seen action against the Creeks, as well as, the British. Their number had been thinned by the fighting and desertion so much so that the number left was not enough to muster a command, and with no officer left to be in charge, Coffee had offered positions in the regular Army. Some took him up on the offer, but most said they would rather go home. Coffee discharged them right there and told them to go home. They were from a group of ten other Kentuckians, going north about nine miles to the east. They hadn't eaten very well on the trek home. Game had been scarce which is why they were so far from the others. They looked hungry.

The Kentuckians had come across Henry and his friend earlier in the day, and they had decided to hunt together. They really didn't know Henry and his friend, and now were sure they didn't want to know them any better.

"Look, this is a big deer. We can split it and you take half back to your friends. Half will feed our boys tonight," Jock said, feeling more charitable now that his side was in control.

"You'd do that for us after what we done?" the first man asked, not sure he had heard right.

"Sure," James said. "Sometimes we haft to help out

when it's needed. Now, you three get this deer cleaned."

"Can we cook a little before leaving? We haven't eaten in two days."

"Yes," James replied, and the men set about building a fire and gutting the deer, hanging it up from a tree by its back legs to drain the blood.

Jock gathered a good-sized snow ball and brought it to William to put on his head. Then he helped William get his jacket back on. He moved close to William and said under his breath, "I wasn't alone out there. I caught a movement out of the corner of my eye, but when I checked, I could see nothing. If there is someone or something out there, we'd better be ready."

William stiffened. "If it was one of theirs, why didn't he come to their aid?" William wondered aloud.

A shrug of the massive shoulders gave William the answer.

William sat holding the snow over the growing bump on the back of his head. The cold seemed to help the pain and the swelling. He watched the butchering. James came and sat beside him. William relayed Jock's warning, and James moved several feet away and sat down on a log. The fire was going good with several pieces of meat spit on sticks stuck in the ground and angled over the fire to cook.

He moved to put his back to a big tree. He was still woozy, and didn't need to be part of what was going on. Jock nodded approval.

"He not feeling too good?" asked one of the Kentuckians. He walked over to William and said, "I'm sorry, young fellow. We were just mighty hungry," as if to make an excuse for their action. William said nothing and just looked at the man. The man hesitated then turned back to his work on the deer carcass.

"Hey, young fellow, you want a piece of roasted venison?" the man asked after checking the spitted meat.

He pulled his hunting knife and cut a big piece from one of the spits and took it over to William. "Wrap your teeth around this. It'll make you feel better."

William accepted the offering, muttering grunted thanks. Jock and James realized that they were hungry, too, as they had not stopped since early morning, and it was now past noon. They helped themselves and then sat down near their rifles but not together. The other men cut pieces of roasted meat and sat down near Henry who was still unconscious. The first man noticed that James, Jock, and William were spread out in a semi-circle facing them with their guns close at hand. His gun was with the others several feet away and unloaded.

William could see that he didn't like this at all. He said, as softly as he could, "We are not alone. Someone or something is out there. I can feel his eyes burning into me." This made the man start to rise.

"Sit still and keep eating. If he were going to attack, he would have by now."

William finished chewing a mouthful of meat. There had been a very slight movement near where Jock was sitting. He called out, "whoever you are come in and have some deer meat."

There was a pause, then suddenly right next to Jock, a big Choctaw Warrior stood up. Jock jumped and moved over. The Warrior wasn't as big as Jock but just as muscled. He drew his knife, strode over to the fire, cut a piece of meat, then stepped back to where Jock was sitting, sat down, and began eating, facing the three men next to the unconscious Henry. He hadn't said a word.

"Well, that's what I like. A man who accepts my invitation to dine and doesn't bore me with a lot of talk," William laughed.

There were soft chuckles all around. The tension had been broken.

"You move like Indian," the Warrior said, turning

toward Jock. This was high praise for the seaman who had never been in the woods before in his life.

"These fellows," Jock responded, pointing at James and William, "taught me."

"That one good shot," grunted the Indian, pointing at William.

"You saw him shoot the deer?" James asked.

"Um, these men," pointing at the Kentuckians and Henry's friend "about to scare deer with too much noise when he shoot," the Indian said.

The three just looked at the Indian uncomfortably, realizing that the Indian had been tracking them. They had been oblivious to his presence. They obviously were not accomplished hunters and woodsmen. One of the Kentucky men said his name was Sam Zimmer from up Beallsville way near Louisburg. He had been a clerk in a store before joining the militia. The other Kentuckian said he had worked for the Blacksmith in Beallsville.

William introduced himself, Jock, and James and explained that they were farmers. If Jock wanted to tell about his past, that was up to him. Jock said nothing. The Choctaw told them his name was Wachecho-a-nee, which he explained means Lone Bear in English.

Seeing Sam's Bearskin Hat, Lone Bear said, "I kill one of those."

"You were at the battle of New Orleans?" Sam asked.

"I fight with Jackson and Coffee. Now go home," Lone Bear replied.

"Where is home?" William asked. There were settlements of Choctaw in Southwestern Tennessee and parts of the Mississippi Territory. From Lone Bear's answer, the best he could figure was somewhere north and west about ten days walk from where they were.

When all of the cooked venison had been eaten, James and Jock helped William to his feet. He admitted he felt a little dizzy, but it was time to leave. The deer had been divided and prepared for carrying. Lone Bear had been given a large chunk of meat from the company's share. They picked up their rifles and turned to leave. Lone Bear had vanished.

"He didn't even say goodbye," James said. "I wonder if we will ever see him again."

They turned to the others. Henry's eyes were open now, and his friend was helping him sit up. Jock told the friend that Henry would probably be a bit wobbly on his feet for a couple of days and that maybe they should stay right where they were. It was a good camp site. Jock steadied William who was also unsteady from the blow to his head.

Henry Schmitt uttered, "You boys will see me again when I will have the advantage."

"You don't learn very well, do you?" Jock replied.

Chapter Nineteen

Discharged

As the militia marched north, Lone Bear appeared at their company's camp several times always bringing meat for the camp. The men became friends.

A week-and-a-half later, the company marched into Nashville, to be immediately disbanded with honorable discharges. The reward of Bounty Land for their service was promised again. It had been promised when they had signed up. More than just a promise had been expected when they mustered out.

Captain Stewart said the men must submit an application for the Bounty Land as soon as Congress passed the bill authorizing the land. He didn't know when that would be. He didn't know how much land would be in the Bounty. For Privates with six months' service and an honorable discharge, he thought it would be 80 acres.

The men grumbled a lot about this because they had been led to believe the Bounty would be 160 acres for each man. Captain Stewart also believed the land to be given as Bounty would be in the Missouri Territory not Tennessee as first thought. There was a lot of misunderstanding about this Bounty Land *promise*. Little did they know, it would take almost forty years to get their Bounty Land.

The morning after their discharge, James, Jock, and William, who were seated behind Blue Belle, started toward Russellville about fifty miles southeast of Nashville. The men were quiet each with their own thoughts. James looked forward to being back with his family. Jock dreamed about starting his new life as a carpenter. Maria Olivarez and the trip to St. Louis occupied William's mind.

Chapter Twenty

Homecoming

The warm afternoon sun felt good on Martha Woods' face. Another peeled potato fell from her hand into the bowl on her lap. Her gaze drifted across the distant tree tops to the hawk making slow circles in the deep blue sky. Slowly, she leaned over to pick another potato from the bag on the porch floor. James' younger sister was enjoying the moderate temperature of the winter-spring transition day. Her eyes returned to the forest. There was a movement in the trees that lined the wagon-path road that passed her farm. It was a horse pulling something, but it was too far off to make it out. On the frontier, everyone needed to be wary of someone or something approaching.

Martha stood up and walked to the edge of the porch. A horse drawn cart emerged from the trees in front of their biggest tobacco field. She could just make out three figures riding on the cart. When it turned into the lane leading to her home, she recognized her brother.

"James is back. James is back, and William is with him," she began, shouting over and over again. She hopped down from the porch and ran toward the cart. Her mother and younger sister came out of the cabin and descended to the front lawn. Her father, hearing the commotion, rushed out of the barn with James' two younger brothers in tow.

James leapt from the sulky before Jock could bring it to a halt. He ran to his sister, wrapping his arms around her, picking her up, and swinging her around in a circle. Then, he ran to his mother and young sister giving them big hugs and kisses. His father got a hug, also. Finally, James picked up in his arms his youngest brother who was about four, and the other brother two years older, got his curly, blond hair tousled.

Jock and William got down from the sulky.

Martha went straight to William taking his hand. "Hello, William. I'm glad you are home safe and sound. I have missed you," she said. She was a year younger than William and very pretty.

"Hello, Martha. It's good to be home," William said.

It occurred to William that Martha had not let go of his hand. Her grip felt strong and firm, not at all like Maria's soft loose grasp when they had held hands in the park. These thoughts had just popped into his head. They surprised and troubled him. Well, Martha had grown up on a farm where everyone worked. He doubted if Maria had worked a day in her life except at her dancing. He didn't have time to think further as the Woods' family surrounded him.

Martha turned toward Jock and waited to be introduced.

James' family greeted William warmly. He even received a hug from James' mother. James introduced Jock to his family who immediately welcomed him to their home. The family members were warm, friendly, happy people. They made everyone feel good to be with them.

James' two, young brothers were full of questions

145

about the war. Their questions tumbled out faster than they could be answered. Did you fight the British? Were you at the battle for New Orleans City? What was the Army like? Did you kill a lot of the enemy? What did you do when you weren't fighting?

James' mother told the boys to slow down. They would get their answers, but first, maybe, the men would like something to drink and to rest on the porch. After all, they had been traveling all day.

Seated on the porch with cups of cold water passed around and also a swig from a jug that James' father produced, James and William began to answer some of the boys' questions. Yes, they had fought in the Battle for New Orleans. William had saved Jock's life, and Jock had saved William's life.

James told of his wound, but they need not worry because it had healed nicely. James' mother gasped and put her hand to her face. James' father looked grim. The only side effect of the wound was some weakness in his hand. The doctor had told him to keep exercising the hand and arm, and eventually the weakness would go away.

Jock listened and answered the questions the family asked. There was some shyness in the big man around people he did not know.

Martha Woods sat right next to William and rarely took her eyes from him. *He noticed that there was a scent of soap from Martha, this being very different from the sweet aroma of Maria. This thought brought the realization of how different the two women were and the comparison he had made.*

The three men did not talk about Maria Olivarez. This subject did not seem like something to be shared at this time.

After about a half hour, William and Jock excused themselves, for William wanted to reach his family's farm before dark. Blue Belle was rested and ready to resume the journey. After goodbyes, William got a little hug from Martha, who told him again that she was glad he was home. *But it had stirred something in him for she had rested her body against his. He passed the hug off to a young girl's enthusiasm.*

Jock took the reins and headed Blue Belle down the lane to the Russell farm.

No one was outside when they drove up to the front of the farm house. William hopped down from the sulky and bounded up the steps to the front door. He entered the large front room. It was empty. He could hear voices coming from the kitchen. The aroma of the cooking dinner filled the room.

Quietly, he walked to the kitchen doorway and entered. His mother and older sister were busy with their backs to the door. They had not heard him drive up or walk into the room. He stood quietly waiting. William's sister Mary turned, started toward the table in the middle of the kitchen, gasped, and froze. Her mother heard the gasp and turned.

"Oh . . . Oh," was all she could say, and she looked as though she might faint.

William quickly took her in his arms and kissed her cheek. "I'm home, Ma."

"William, you scared me to death . . . don't do that to me," she said with a little smile. "I've got to sit down," and went to a chair and sat down.

Mary gave William a big hug and kiss on the cheek and was about to say something when she stopped, staring at the huge man who more than filled the doorway.

"Mother . . . Mary, meet my good friend Jock Smith. Jock, this is my mother, Sarah Russell and my sister, Mary. Jock was with James and me at the Battle for New Orleans. Jock saved my life," William shared.

Jock entered the room, and the room suddenly became smaller. He bowed to William's mother and to

Mary saying how happy he was to meet them. "William has told me so much about you that I feel like I know you already."

Sarah Russell made Jock feel right at home. He was welcome in her home forever. Mary did not say much; she just watched the big man.

"I believe your father and brothers are in the South field getting it ready for planting. They should be home any minute now because it's almost dinner time," said his mother.

"I invited Jock to come home with me for a while before starting his carpentry business," William explained.

"You are welcome to stay with us for as long as you like, Jock," Sarah Russell agreed.

Some distant voices came through the half-open Dutch door. One young voice questioned, "I wonder whose horse and cart that is in front of our house?"

"I don't know. I don't recognize the rig," they heard an older voice respond.

William walked out the back door to squeals of recognition from his young brothers.

"William's back . . . William's back," and they rushed to greet him.

Shaking hands, his father said, "It's good to have you home, Son."

The boys, suddenly silent, stood looking at the big man who had followed William out the door.

"Father, I'd like you to meet my very good friend Jock Smith," William said. "Jock was with James and me and fought at our side."

William Russell Sr., extended his hand, "Jock, welcome to our home."

William then introduced the boys to Jock. Jock put the boys at ease immediately. His big, warm smile and friendly manner cured their timidity.

The men stood and talked for a few minutes about the trip back from New Orleans.

"We better not stay out here talking. Whatever you tell me will need to be repeated to your mother and sister, so we better go inside."

It was getting dark and William thought about Blue Belle. "Can we put Jock's horse and sulky in the barn?" William asked.

"Yes, there's an empty stall that he can use, and there's plenty of space at the back of the barn for the sulky," William's father answered. "Why don't you boys help Mr. Smith with his horse."

They all walked around to the front of the house to unload the sulky before taking it to the barn.

Jock told William to go inside with his father so that he and the boys could take care of Blue Belle. Jock and Blue Belle, with the brothers riding the sulky, headed for the barn.

William and his father went into the house.

The dinner table was spread with a red and white calico table cloth. There were benches on each side of the table and chairs at each end. The room was well-lit with several lamps. When they sat down for dinner, Mary asked Jock to sit next to her so she could hear all about the war and their adventures.

William and Jock told of the war and Army life. Some comparisons were made to William Sr.'s experiences in George Washington's Army. They talked of the trip to Tennessee. When James' wound was mentioned, William's mother visibly paled. She was glad he was alright now. The subject of Maria Olivarez again was avoided. William would talk to his father and mother about her later. He would explain about his promise to Maria's mother.

Neither William nor Jock missed the look that passed between the adult Russells when William mentioned the trouble in the woods with Henry Schmitt. Nor did they miss Sarah's slight hand movement to stop further discussion of Henry Schmitt nor the quick glance at the young Russells. The discussion of Henry would also be saved until later.

Chapter Twenty-One

Russellville

During the evening meal, William's family told Jock of the founding of Russellville.

William Sr. and Nathan, his brother, had brought their families to this part of Tennessee in 1786. Three other families had come with them. At that time, there were no settlements west of Maryville until Nashborough some 90 miles farther west.

The Cherokee, Shawnee, and Chickasaw tribes hunted the area, but because the tribes were always warring between themselves, they had never established permanent settlements. During the Revolutionary War, the Indians, incited by the British, had attacked the American settlements driving many settlers to safer areas in Kentucky.

The road from Maryville had been just a wide, dirt path used by the buffalo and Indians. The trail followed the topography of the land. Buffalo always took the easiest way to push through the dense brush and forest. Being herd animals, they often moved two, three, or even four abreast. This movement of animals caused their trails to be wider than a foot path.

Some of the trails were ancient. Those had been created by the Mammoths and Giant Deer that roamed the forest a thousand years ago, as they moved from one feeding ground to another.

These trails crisscrossed the land from the Gulf of Mexico to the Great Lakes. Those animal and Indian trails eventually became used by the early explorers. When the settlers arrived, they also used the trails. Later, armies followed the well-worn trails as they defended the settlers. The armies and settlers often widened the trails for wagons to pass.

It was a trail such as this that William Sr. and Nathan followed to find their land. They improved the trail to allow their wagons to pass.

Nathan Russell had surmised: "If we make the road passable, other people will come. Also, we will need the road to haul in supplies and ship out our tobacco, cotton, and other crops."

Many of the men that came to Tennessee were veterans of the Revolutionary War and had applied for and received Bounty Land Grants from the Federal Government for their service. William, Sr. and Nathan Russell had both joined the American Army in 1777 when the British invaded Virginia. The political realities of the British tyranny were well known to the brothers. Independence from England was the only answer. Both men had been in several major engagements including: Brandywine, Camden, and the siege at Yorktown.

Nathan Russell, wounded in the thigh by a musket ball at the battle of Camden, now walked with a slight limp. After getting wounded, he had returned to the family farm in western Virginia to recover. Then, he returned to the Army for the last few months of the war.

The Russells had selected land southwest of Knoxville in a long valley cut by the small, Blue River.

William's father had received a grant for 320 acres because he was a Sergeant and had served in the Army for five years. William's uncle Nathan had received 160 acres as a private with two-and-a-half years of service. Nathan Russell had taken twenty of his acres for the settlement of Russellville. Nathan's other 140 acres adjoined William Sr.'s farm. The two men worked the farms together.

The men of the other three families--Miron Adams, Jeremy Alexander, and Samuel Johnson--were also veterans and had fought beside the Russell brothers. Each had at least one Land Grant. William's father and uncle had helped the other men to get the Land Grants because they both could read and write.

Miron Adams used his land grant to start a modest farm. Because Miron had been raised on a tobacco plantation where his father had been the overseer, he chose his primary crop to be tobacco. His father had been bound to the owner of the plantation for ten years. His mother, a bond servant in the owner's house, had fallen for the overseer. The plantation owner, a good man, allowed them to marry. Miron had come along a year later.

After the bond was worked off, his father had stayed with the owner. His father had not been interested in having land of his own. Working for someone else was just fine. Miron, however, longed for his own land. When war came, he joined because he believed in the cause. The Bounty Land offered for service would be a bonus opportunity, so he took advantage of it.

Miron brought with him Maggie, his wife, and their two children--a boy, Steven, ten years old and a girl, Catherine, seven years old. Sadly, they had lost another girl to disease the year before their move to Tennessee.

Miron also brought six slaves: Jim, Miron's trusted Overseer, and his wife, Betty, who helped Maggie with the children and around the house. The other four slaves included three field hands and a woman who would help wherever she was needed.

Jeremy Alexander wasn't much for farming, so he bargained with William's uncle for a place next to The Trading Post to build and operate a Tavern. Incidentally, Jeremy made a pretty good whiskey. Jeremy's wife, Alice, cooked for the patrons of the Tavern. The Bounty Land he received from the government, he sold to William's father.

Samuel Johnson also started a farm on his Bounty Land. He wanted to raise horses. He brought with him two brood mares and a stallion. He put in a large field of hay to feed the horses during the winter. With the help of the men of the settlement, he built a large barn for the horses. His wife also was a good horse woman and helped him with the care and maintenance of the stock.

Indians came through the settlement, stopping at The Trading Post to trade furs for goods they needed, including powder and shot. The Cherokee were the largest population in the area. In fact, it was the Cherokee land that the Federal government was giving to the veterans. They were not happy to see the white settlers. Sometimes they caused trouble, attacking small farms and stealing cattle and horses- anything they could get their hands on. In spite of the Indian trouble, settlers continued to move into the area.

As neighbors did at that time, everyone helped build the cabins and the barns for the new people. Cabin raisings and barn raisings were causes for celebration. In the wilderness, there weren't many occasions for community. People used raisings as an occasion to get together and have fun.

Russellville had been built on a bluff overlooking the Blue River. The bluff was high enough so that the spring floods would not wash it away. The settlers had been mindful of the flood problems and built their homes accordingly.

Nathan Russell also had started a freight-hauling business to supply the westerners. He hauled their grain, cotton, and tobacco to Knoxville to sell to buyers from back East. His Trading Post was the center of the village. In the beginning, The Trading Post and Jeremy's Tavern were the only buildings in Russellville. But Russellville had grown, and by the time William had gotten home, the settlement proudly claimed twenty-six buildings. They included a livery stable, a blacksmith shop, the Hogs Head Tavern with a couple of rooms in back for travelers and a barn, Forgert's Seed and Grain store, a freight office, the Doctor's cabin, several log cabins where people lived, and Nathan's house.

Nathan Russell's home was impressive not because of its size but because it was frame, not log. William's uncle had hauled the lumber for the house from the sawmill over by Maryville, about thirty-five miles away. This house fulfilled a promise he had made to Lydia, his wife. He had promised he would build her a proper home as soon as his business got going. Within six months the house had been started and finished before the year ended.

William Sr. had picked out a good piece of land for farming that was not too heavily forested. The land was fertile and good for growing just about any crop. William's father planted corn, cotton, and tobacco.

Chapter Twenty-Two

The Schmitt Incident

When dinner was over and William's young brothers had been sent to bed, the adults gathered around the big fireplace in the main room to talk for a while before going to bed themselves. Work begins very early on a farm, so they would not stay up too long.

William Sr. asked about his son's encounter with Henry Schmitt. William recounted the three meetings: on the battle line, on the New Orleans street, and in the Mississippi forest. The expressions on the faces of the adult Russells grew grave.

When William finished, his father (who always called himself "William Sr." in the retelling) told the story of what he referred to as "The Schmitt Incident." It happened about two weeks before William and Jock arrived. William's father had gone into Russellville to see his brother and pick up some seed grain for the spring planting.

******

William Sr. and Nathan were talking in Nathan's store when they had heard the crack of a whip and a cry of pain. Looking out the window, they had seen Benjamin Schmitt and that not-too-bright son of his riding down the road. In front of them chained hand and foot, was Jim, Miron Adams' slave. As they watched, Jim stumbled and Benjamin flicked Jim's back with his whip. Jim cried out again.

William Sr. later would say, "If I'd thought about it, I might not have acted as hastily as I did. I knew Schmitt's reputation as a brutal and dirty fighter who likes to beat men up. I knew of his sadistic streak and his work as a slave catcher and his reputation as a slave abuser, often returning the caught slaves with bloodied backs and legs. But, I couldn't sit still with Jim being whipped."

The man with the whip, Benjamin Schmitt, had a hard, mean look about him. The scars on his face told of fights he had been in. Although short in stature, his barrel chest and thick arms were intimidating. His favorite tactic was to wrap his arms around a man and crush the man's lungs. He had scars on the top of his head that could be seen through his thin, black hair. He used head butts to knock his opponent off balance enough to get a fight-ending bear hug. Fighting made him feel superior to the men he beat. On the few occasions that he lost, he would hold a grudge. With some help from his sons, he was not above ambushing the man who beat him.

William Sr. ran out of the store and pulled Benjamin Schmitt from his horse. "That's enough! Miron Adams doesn't want his property damaged."

"You watch yourself, Russell," Schmitt yelled. "I'm within my rights. I know the law when it comes to catching slaves. I don't tolerate no interference with my slave catching." With that he swung a powerful, right hook at William Sr.'s face. All Schmitt hit was air.

William Sr. had stepped back and to the left. He smashed a hard right jab to Schmitt's jaw, sending him sprawling face down in the dirt. Schmitt got to his feet spitting blood. Cursing, he charged, arms outstretched, for a fight-ending bear hug. William Sr. met the charge with another right jab this time to Schmitt's nose--breaking it.

Furious, Schmitt got up. "You got me with two lucky punches. Now, you're going to pay."

William Sr. didn't answer. He stood ready. He was no stranger to fist fighting. In the Army he had learned how to fight and defend himself. He also had taught other men how to fight with their fists. Schmitt's reputation for squeezing the air out of a man's lungs was known to him. He was not about to let Benjamin get near him.

The other rider, Schmitt's oldest son, had moved over and was pawing at a pistol in his belt.

"You pull that pistol and you're a dead man." Nathan Russell stood on the store's porch holding a rifle. "Now, with your other hand pull the pistol out and drop it."

Schmitt's son did as he was told.

Benjamin Schmitt, with a shout, charged again, anger in his eyes and blood running from his nose. He shifted from side-to-side trying to avoid another blow. William Sr. grabbed both arms above the elbows, put his foot in Schmitt's belly, and rolled backwards, flipping Schmitt high in the air. Schmitt landed on his back, knocking the wind out of him. He got up slowly, gasping for air. William Sr. waited. Schmitt would be very cautious now.

William Sr. was not about to stand toe-to-toe and slug it out with Schmitt. He moved gradually to his left. Schmitt turned to face him. Slowly, William Sr. circled. Schmitt stood ready. Unexpectedly, the sunlight hit Schmitt's eyes, jamming his view. This momentary blindness was the advantage William Sr. had been maneuvering to get. He slammed a right into Schmitt's face. Schmitt connected with a left to William Sr.'s head. Several blows were exchanged. Then, William Sr. landed a hard right jab to Schmitt's Adam's apple, and Schmitt sat down hard, coughing and trying to catch his breath.

"Stay down, Schmitt," William Sr. commanded. "This is one fight you are not going to win."

Hatred covered Schmitt's face, but he stayed sitting in the dirt. The fight was over.

An angry voice came from where the slave Jim stood.

"What right have you got to whip my slave?" Miron Adams demanded.

"You've whipped him so badly that he won't be any good for a month. He's not a runaway. He was picking up a horse for me." Miron ordered. "Now, take these chains off him!"

Schmitt growled back as he got up, blood dripping from his nose and mouth, "He didn't have no pass. That makes him a runaway. You owe me money for bringing him back."

"Like Hell I do. He did have a permit. I wrote it for him myself. And where's my horse?" Miron questioned.

Jim, said, "Master Miron, the other one is riding your horse," pointing to the man who had thought about pulling a pistol.

"This is my horse," the younger Schmitt claimed.

"You're a liar," Miron snarled, "Mr. Russell, please look in the horse's left ear. Does it say MA02?"

Looking in the horse's left ear, William's father replied, "That's what it says."

"You better get down, fellow. You're on Mr. Adams' horse."

The younger Schmitt complied.

"Is this your saddle and bridle, Miron?" William Sr. said, as he lifted the flap holding the stirrup and saw burned into the leather *Miron Adams*. And tucked in a small pocket was a piece of paper which William Sr. removed. He read it aloud so all who were watching the proceedings could hear.

"The bearer of this permit is my man Jim. He is off my property to pick up a horse from Byron Adams and

return it to me. Please give him safe passage.
Signed: Miron Adams"

Benjamin Schmitt pulled a key from his pocket and started to remove the chains. He dropped the wrist irons on Jim's foot.

"Ouhooooo," moaned Jim.

"The Sheriff is going to hear of this. You're a liar, a horse thief, and you damaged my property. You better get out of town and don't ever come back. And take those things with you," Miron ordered, kicking the chains toward Benjamin Schmitt.

Benjamin picked up the chains muttering, "You owe me money."

"I don't owe you a cent. Now, get out of here," Miron yelled at him.

Schmitt's son brought Benjamin's horse over and Benjamin mounted. The son climbed on behind, and they started down the road going out of the village. They looked back once.

Benjamin shouted, "You owe me money." Then, they rode out of sight.

"Will you help me get Jim here over to the doctor's office?" Miron asked.

They helped Jim walk to the cabin that the doctor used as an office and home. The doctor was really more of an animal doctor than a human doctor. He cleaned the cuts with whiskey and then rubbed some kind of salve on them. Jim winced a few times but said little during the treatment.

"Jim, how did this happen?" Miron asked.

"I no runaway, Master Miron."

"I know, Jim," Miron said.

"I was headed home from Mr. Byron's when those men stopped me. They asked me where I was going, and I told them here to Russellville because that's where my master lives. 'I got a pass,' I says, and I reached for the paper. The younger one hit me with a pistol on the side of my head and knocked me off the horse. He said I was a runaway and not to lie. They put the chains on me and made me walk here."

"Can you ride? We need to get you home where Betty can look after you."

Miron and Jim rode away slowly so as not to jiggle Jim too much. They left William Sr. standing in the street watching them leave.

"Miron, you watch out. That Benjamin Schmitt is a bad one. He may try to get back at you," warned William Sr.

"You better watch yourself, too. You beat him badly, and he's not one to forget," Miron called back.

Miron and Jim disappeared around a bend. William Sr. went back to Nathan's store.

Nathan stood waiting in front of the door. He said he hoped they had seen the last of the Schmitts. William Sr. agreed and prepared to leave with the supplies he had come for.

Describing the incident in detail, Nathan Russell wrote a letter to the Sheriff. He also wrote a letter stating Miron Adams' charges against Benjamin Schmitt for abusing Jim and trying to steal the Adams' horse.

The Sheriff had gone out to see Schmitt about the charges. Except the fight with William Sr., Schmitt denied everything because his face still showed the bruises and cut marks from William Sr.'s fists. Benjamin claimed that Jim was a runaway and had not been able to show a pass. Also, he claimed that Miron Adams had refused to pay for the slave's return. His son verified the father's story. Because the horse was returned and whipping a runaway was not a crime, the Sheriff could not arrest Benjamin.

William Sr. ended his story with: "And that ends the story of The Schmitt Incident."

161

Chapter Twenty-Three

The Warning

March had come to Tennessee like a lion with snow, cold temperatures and lots of rain. Now, the warm, sunny lamb days would finish April and usher in May. The soil of the fields had dried enough to be turned over and made ready for planting. William and his father with the help of his two brothers worked from dawn to dusk plowing and clearing rocks and debris from the fields. Jock spent his days repairing winter damage to the barn and building a new birthing and shearing shed for the sheep.

Worry about the Benjamin Schmitt threats slipped into the background.

William told his family about Maria Olivarez, his promise to her mother, and his planned trip to St. Louis to find Maria. Jock and William's sister, Mary, were beginning to find lots to talk about in the evenings. Lone Bear came to the farm on his way to a Choctaw council meeting.

After a couple of weeks passed without hearing any more from the Schmitts, William's father decided it would be safe to go to Knoxville with the freight wagons.

He had purchased another one hundred acres from a veteran with some bounty land and wanted to record the deed. William and Jock were at the farm now, so they could handle any trouble.

Three days after his father left, William and Jock were working in the barn on the sulky, getting it ready for the trip to St. Louis. Jock was adding a storage box under the seat. The box would be large enough to carry food and bedrolls and to keep them dry if it rained.

William leaned against Blue Belle's stall, alternating his attention between Jock and Blue Belle. She lowered her head to the hay bin for another mouthful of fresh hay. William watched her chew. The sounds of her large, back molars grinding the hay filled the barn. William saw her ears flip forward as she turned to look toward the rear of the barn. Then, he turned to see what she saw. Lone Bear was standing there.

"Your horse hear good. The Schmitts, they come," he said.

William and Jock listened to Lone Bear as he explained of coming upon the Schmitt camp somewhere north of the Cumberland River. He recognized Henry Schmitt among the men in the camp. Fortunately, Lone Bear had gotten close enough to hear their conversation. They were talking about the Russell family and an Adams family and how they were going to get even with the two families. There were five men in the camp: Henry, Henry's friend from the deer incident, a short, older man with thin, black hair, and two other men.

Lone Bear had been unable hear the specific details of what the Schmitts were planning. However, he had heard enough to know they were coming after William, his father, and someone named Miron Adams. Lone Bear had followed them the next day. The Schmitts had gone to an old, poorly-kept, farm. There had been a board nailed to a fence post with the word Schmitt painted on it. The

Schmitts had stayed there three days; then, they saddled up and started south.

Lone Bear had followed until he was certain that they were headed toward Russellville. Then, he came ahead to warn William and Jock.

"How long before the Schmitts get here?" William asked. Neither he nor Jock had brought their rifles to the barn.

"Three . . . four hours, maybe. They were on horses," the Indian replied.

"Come on, Jock, we need to get our rifles and warn Mother and Mary. Lone Bear, come into the house," invited William, and they started for the house.

"I stay here and watch. Give warning if they come," Lone Bear answered and climbed to the hay loft.

Jock sprinted to the back door ahead of William. Both men were in and the door closed in a few seconds. The two women looked up from their work in the kitchen, startled at the rush inside by Jock and William.

"What . . .?" William's mother didn't finish the question. The look on her son's face said trouble, and Jock's going straight to his weapons in the living room spoke volumes. She waited for an explanation.

"Where are the boys?" William asked.

"On the front porch playing," Mary answered. She hurried to the front door and called them inside. These were pioneer women. They knew when action needed to be quick and decisive. Protesting, the boys came in. One look at the grave faces of the adults, and the boys went silent and waited. Mary took down one of the rifles from its place on the wall and checked its load. She primed the pan with powder. Setting the rifle in a handy position, she took down the other rifle and prepared it to fire. Mary knew firearms. Her father had made sure of that, and she was a good shot.

"The Schmitts are coming after father and the

family," William said, as calmly as he could. "They are also coming after Miron Adams and his family. Lone Bear just brought the warning. He is in the barn watching."

The back door opened and Lone Bear stepped inside.

"See nothing, but I have feeling we are being watched from the woods over there," he said, pointing to where the forest began on the other side of the road that ran in front of the farm. The place he pointed was about two hundred feet from the house.

Freshly plowed fields bordered the path that led from the road to the house. The field to the west of the house had also been plowed.

The Russell's two-story, log house had been built on a native stone foundation. Under the kitchen dug deep in the ground was a room with shelves for food storage. Also, under one side of the kitchen, a well had been dug so water could be pumped without going outside. This "inside" well was an innovation William's father had seen in New England during the war.

The Russell farm boasted two wells. The second well was behind the barn. It was used to water the stock. The little house was nowhere near either of the wells.

The house made a good fort with food and water available without leaving the building. There were no hiding places on three of its sides. The back door and one window of the house faced the front of the barn. A large Oak tree stood on the west side of the backyard. A rope swing for the boys was hung from a big branch.

The barn, however, being a short distance from the house, would be a good place to stage an attack. Behind the barn was a large pasture and beyond that was a sizeable, wooded area. Lone Bear had used the wooded area to approach the barn and had caught William and Jock by surprise. None of the horses were grazing in the pasture this day because of the previous night's rain. The horses had been brought into the barn so they would not be out in bad weather.

"We need to warn Miron Adams," William explained. "I need to get my horse. Lone Bear, do you think you could come with me to the barn and guard the approach from the woods?"

"What if the Schmitts have sent someone into the barn? Lone Bear could be shot before he even gets to the barn," Mary added, thinking out loud.

"I have been watching the barn from the door. There has been no movement," Lone Bear replied. "I go in the open window. The horse there has poked his head out several times and seems undisturbed."

"We need a distraction," Jock said, returning to the kitchen. "I have been watching the woods over across the road, and there has been no movement. If the Schmitts are over there, something we do might give William and Lone Bear the chance they need to get to the barn."

"Mother and I can go out on the porch with rifles and walk over to the side away from the barn," Mary suggested. "Then, Jock, you follow a minute later with your rifle and come to where we are. This will draw their attention. William and Lone Bear can run for the barn."

Jock didn't like exposing Mary or her Mother and said so. There had to be a better way, but a decision had to be made before any more time passed.

William's Mother made the decision. "Brian, please come down here," she said, addressing the oldest boy. The boys had been sent upstairs for their protection.

She continued "Samuel, you stay up there. Mary has a good plan. If we keep moving and only stay outside long enough for your brother and Lone Bear to get to the barn, we will be alright. Brian, you will watch through the back window and let us know when William and Lone Bear reach the barn. We will come right back in then."

The two women picked up their rifles and stood by

the front door. Jock stood right behind them. Brian went to the rear window with a pistol. He was a good shot with rifle or pistol. His father had taught him well.

"Are you ready, William . . . Lone Bear?" William's Mother asked.

Each nodded yes.

William's Mother pulled open the front door and stepped onto the porch with her rifle at the ready. Mary followed and both women walked to the side of the porch. Jock stepped out and went to their side. William and Lone Bear were out the door and sprinting toward the barn.

As they reached the point-of-no-return, two men emerged from the woods running toward the barn. On the run, Lone Bear raised his rifle and fired at the men. The ball hit the dirt in front of them. They turned and ran back to the woods. William dove in through the big doors, rolled, and ran to the back door. He raised his gun and fired as the men disappeared into the trees.

Quickly, he saddled the big chestnut stallion. He was the fastest horse the Russells owned, and William needed all the speed he could get. Lone Bear reloaded both rifles and watched the woods. William climbed into the saddle and took his rifle from Lone Bear. With a whoop he slammed his heels into the horse's flanks. The stallion reached top speed as he charged out the barn door. Turning, William raced the horse down the path beside the plowed field. The path was parallel to the road. A shot rang out behind him, and a dirt clod flew into the air beside him. Then, he and the stallion plunged into the woods on a game trail that led to the road and to the Adams' farm. He had gotten away clean.

William galloped into the Adams' front yard. Mrs. Adams had heard him coming and had come out the front door.

"Where is Mr. Adams?" William shouted, as he pulled the stallion to a halt.

"He is in the north field with Jim pulling stumps," she answered. "What is wrong?"

"The Schmitts are back. They attacked our farm," William yelled, as the big horse leapt toward the north field. "Get inside and protect yourself. I'll warn Mr. Adams."

"Oh . . . Oh . . . Hurry!" She yelled with panic in her voice. She was not as strong as his mother or sister. She would not handle this crisis well.

As he approached the field, he could see he was too late. Miron Adams lay on his back. Jim lay nearby face down in the dirt. He could see the dark red stains where two bullets had entered Miron's body. Jim had a big red blotch on his back. William rode close to see if either man was breathing. Neither man moved. They were dead.

William turned his horse toward Russellville and help. The stallion galloped up to the trading post, and slid to a stop. Several people saw William and started running to learn what had happened.

Nathan Russell looked up from helping Mrs. Alexander, as William ran into the store. Surprised, Nathan asked, "What's going on?"

"The Schmitts are back. They have killed Miron Adams and Jim. They attacked our farm. We need some help."

Two men had come in behind William. Jeremy Alexander and the Doctor heard the last part.

"Who killed Miron Adams?" Jeremy asked.

"I believe it was the Schmitts," William answered, as he tried to suck in air.

"You men, get your guns and go after the murderers." Mrs. Alexander ordered. "I'll get Mrs. Russell and the Doc's wife, and we'll go help Mrs. Adams." She left, almost running.

"We need as many men as we can get to go after the killers. Go get your guns and your horses and whatever you need to be on their trail for two or three days. We'll meet in front of the tavern," Nathan instructed. "Jeremy, see if any of the men in the tavern will join us."

Chapter Twenty-Four

Hunt for the Killers

William didn't wait for the men; he rode to the field where Miron Adams and Jim lay. Standing about fifty feet from the bodies was Lone Bear with one of William's father's horses. The Indian had ridden bareback. William sent a questioning look at Lone Bear.

"After you get away," he said, "the men that shoot at you get their horses and ride out of the woods going south on the road. The men behind the barn must have seen the others leave because they ran their horses across the field and followed the others down the road. I borrowed this horse and followed them until they were past James' farm. They were moving fast. They knew you would be bringing men to hunt them. Jock stayed with the women. I come here to find you."

As William got down from his horse, he thanked Lone Bear.

"I'm going to figure out what happened here." William could read signs better than most and what had happened was very clear to anyone really looking. Miron Adams had hitched a horse to a stump. Then, with Jim urging the horse forward and Miron chopping the roots, the stump had been pulled almost free.

Two men had ridden out of the woods behind the stump. They walked their horses up to about ten feet of the working men. At some point Miron and Jim must have heard the two men approaching and turned to face them. There was some conversation because the horses had remained in one place for several minutes.

Miron Adams had been shot twice, once in the chest and once in the gut. Jim had run toward the house. But before he had raced twenty feet, he had been shot in the back. After the shootings one of the riders had gotten down and walked over to Adams' body, knelt, and searched it.

William's anger rose. He knew who had killed Adams. There on the ground was a left boot, heel print with a curved-cut. He had seen this print before in the Mississippi forest where he had shot a deer. The heel print was made by Henry Schmitt's boot. William stuck some sticks in the ground around the footprints and around several of the horse's hoof prints so no one would destroy this evidence before the others could see this proof.

The other rider had ridden to Miron Adams' harnessed horse and unhitched it, leading it back to the woods. That man rode a horse with a crossed shoe.

"Lone Bear, did the men who rode out of the woods have an extra horse?" William asked.

"No, only the horses they were on," was Lone Bear's reply.

"They got smart. They realized if they were caught with Adams' horse, they would be tied to the murders. I'll bet it killed old Benjamin Schmitt to leave Adams' horse behind. We'll probably find it somewhere along their trail," William surmised.

The sound of riders and a wagon arriving turned the two men toward the farm. There were three women in the wagon that pulled up in front of the Adams' home. They immediately got down and went into the house.

Nathan Russell, Jeremy Alexander, the Doctor, and five other men from the village rode to where William and Lone Bear waited. William introduced Lone Bear to the men who didn't know him. Then, he told what the signs said about the murderers and who had worn the boot with the curve-cut heel that made the print beside Miron's body. All the men looked at the boot print and the hoof prints that William had staked out. The Doctor said he would remove the bullets for the Sheriff to see.

Lone Bear agreed with William's descriptions of the murderers. Then, he added, "six men ride out of the woods headed southwest on the road. I got this horse and followed to be sure they were leaving. I returned to Russell farm and told Jock and the women. Jock asked me to come here to find William. I see the murdered men and then look for signs to tell who did this. The boot print with curve scar on heel belongs to Henry Schmitt. In the Mississippi forest, I see this mark before."

A call for the Doctor came from one of the women at the house. The Doctor got on his horse and rode to the front door, dismounted, and walked in. Mrs. Adams was hysterical with grief. Mrs. Russell, Mrs. Alexander, and the Doctor's wife all tried to comfort her. The Adams' young children stood around not fully understanding what had happened.

Betty, Jim's wife, was crying in the kitchen. Her children and the other black woman were with her.

The Doctor made some tea for Mrs. Adams and Betty. He said an Indian Medicine Man had taught him this remedy. The tea, made from dried plants that he had gathered from around Russellville, would help to calm the women.

The men carried Miron Adams into the house and laid him on the table to be made ready for burial. The

Adams' three field hands carried Jim's body to the small cabin where he and Betty lived. Betty with the other black woman went to the cabin to ready Jim for burial.

Jock brought William's mother and sister to the Adams' home in his sulky. The boys rode standing up in the cargo box Jock had added. Then, with another man from Russellville, Jock went to the barn and began building two coffins.

In the meantime, William and Lone Bear had begun tracking the killers. They followed the tracks to a spot in the woods well back from the road and opposite the front of the Russell farm. They found the Adams' horse tied to a tree. The horse was happy to see William and Lone Bear. The murderers had met four other riders there.

Dismounting, the men had crept through the trees and underbrush to a place where they could easily see the Russell house and barn. Again, William and Lone Bear found the boot print with the curved-cut in the heel.

Two of the men had retrieved their horses and ridden off through the woods to the southwest. These were probably the men who had been behind the barn and who had gone far enough to be able to cross the road and work their way back unseen to the rear of the barn.

The men facing the front of the farm house had lain in the bushes for some time because the grass was still flattened where their bodies had been. They had a good view of the house and barn. The only obstruction was the large Oak tree in the yard on the right side. The branches had been cut high up so a horse could be ridden underneath. Two chairs made of branches in the Adirondack style were under the tree.

William and Lone Bear rode out of the woods onto the road in front of the Russell farm leading the Adams' horse. Nathan Russell, Jeremy Alexander, and the men from the village were just coming into sight. Lone Bear waited for the men. William led the horse to the back pasture and released him there. William returned to Lone Bear's side at the same time his uncle and the other men got there.

Quickly, he filled in the men on what he and Lone Bear had found.

"You two scout ahead. We will follow a short distance back," his uncle said.

The scouts, following an easy-to-read trail, were able to keep a fast pace. After over six miles, William halted at the side of the road. Two riders had turned off on an old game trail that angled straight south. Jeremy Alexander and another man, Jason Brightweather, from the village would follow this trail with William. Lone Bear and the other men from Russellville would continue following the four remaining riders.

William was happy he had Jeremy with him, not that he was a woodsman but he was good in a fight. He had served three years in the Continental Army with his father and was well known for stopping fights in his tavern quickly--with a right or left hook that men did not get up from.

Jason Brightweather, William had only talked with a couple of times. Brightweather seemed competent. Jeremy knew him much better and said he was glad Jason was with them because he was a good shot. Jason and his wife owned a small farm north of the Blue River. William estimated Jason to be about five years older than he.

They followed the trail as fast as they could. It switched from trail to trail; slowly a pattern began to emerge. The riders were turning east. Were they going back to the farm or to Russellville? The men stopped to consider this new information. Perhaps, one of them should go back and warn the other men and the people at the Adams' farm while William continued following the trail. Jeremy volunteered to return to spread the warning.

William and Jason continued on the trail. There were

about two hours of daylight remaining. It would be very hard to follow the riders' trail that night because there would be no moon, and dark clouds were rolling in from the west threatening rain. If it rained, the trail would be wiped out.

They had just come around a bend in the trail when Jason suddenly stopped.

"William, they know we are following. The rider on the horse with the crossed shoe stopped here and turned to check his back trail. See, his horse stood sideways to the trail while the rider looked back then hurried on."

William had missed that sign completely. He was rushing to catch the men they were following when he should have been slower and more cautious. A mistake like that could have been fatal.

"The rider could just be looking over his back trail so that he would know what it looked like if he returned on the same path. In the deep woods it was always a good idea to check the back trail often so that it would be familiar if the route must be retraced. Also, it was good to know whether or not someone might be following. Men on the run should always be looking behind them," Jason commented. "This man sat here watching for several minutes."

Jason was good, and he wasn't relying completely on William. Being independently focused was even better, William thought.

The trees around the trail in front of them thinned out forming a sizable open area. They had an unobstructed view for a good distance. Very little brush grew on either side of the trail. On the other end of the opening, the trail disappeared into thick brush where a tree had fallen across the trail. It looked like a good place for an ambush.

An uncomfortable feeling stirred in William's gut. Keeping his horse between himself and the potential ambush spot, he dismounted. "Let's back up; we're too exposed here," William murmured in a hushed tone.

As Jason started to climb down, there was a shot, and a rifle ball passed through the branches near where his head had been. Both men quickly pulled their horses back around the bend in the trail and into the thick brush and trees beside the trail. William had glanced down the trail just in time to see the smoke from the rifle dissipate in the tree branches above the deadfall.

William estimated the distance to the thick growth of trees and the deadfall to be about two-hundred feet. Someone would need to be a very good shot to hit anything at that range, particularly a moving target like a man.

When they were well back from the trail and could not be seen, William whispered, "I will circle around and try to get behind them. Jason, wait here with the horses and keep an eye on that deadfall. That is where I saw the rifle smoke."

William started moving directly perpendicular to the trail. Slowly and quietly, he made a big circle coming up behind where he thought the ambusher had waited. On his stomach he approached to a point where he could see behind the deadfall. No one was waiting, but the grass was matted down. Someone had been waiting there. On the deadfall something white drew his attention.

William backed up and scouted farther. The men might be waiting some other place. Staying deep in the woods, he took his time working his way in a circle around the ambush spot. He approached the deadfall from a different angle but found no sign of the Schmitts. As he worked his way around behind the deadfall, he found where their horses had been tied. Their trail went off to the east.

After satisfying himself that the ambushers had gone, he followed their trail to a small brook. The crossed shoe print was plainly visible. These men had made no attempt to cover their tracks. They seemed a little too sure of themselves, and that made William angry. The riders knew he was a good tracker and would be able to follow them. The two horses had entered the water but had not gone out the other side. He found a rock that had been turned over by a passing hoof. The men had gone down stream. The brook ran north toward the Holston River. It would be pointless to try to follow them now. It would be dark soon, and it was about to start raining which would wash away where the riders left the brook.

Returning to the deadfall, he saw the cut heel print of Henry Schmitt's boot. The white spot he had noticed earlier was a folded piece of paper wedged into the bark of the old tree. It read:

Saw you Cheater sorry we can't wait.

See you soon.

It had no signature.

William walked down the trail to where Jason waited with the horses.

"Let's head back. They got away from us. They were waiting, but when we didn't ride into their trap, they left," William said and showed Jason the note and explained what he had found. The two men mounted and returned in the direction they had come. By the time they reached the road, it was dark and a soft rain had started to fall.

When they got back to the farm, his Uncle Nathan and Aunt Lydia Russell, Jock, his mother, sister, brothers, and Lone Bear were there. Jason was invited to stay the night. He accepted because the rain had really started coming down. Jason's oilskin had helped to keep the rain from completely soaking them. They put their horses in the barn, rubbed them dry, and gave them some hay. When William and Jason entered the back door, they inhaled the delicious aromas of meat and bread cooking.

While they ate, William's uncle told of the capture of one of the attackers whose horse had gone lame. The

Schmitts had gone off and left both the man and the lame horse. Deserted, the man turned into the woods to lose the pursuers. Lone Bear saw the tracks and found the man on foot trying to hide. The man turned out to be Henry's Army friend who was none too happy with the Schmitts for leaving him. It didn't take much persuasion to get the names of the other men who were in the attack group.

William and Jason had been following Henry Schmitt and his father Benjamin. The other four men were Benjamin's brother Kurt, his son Fritz, Henry's not-too-bright brother Heinz, and Henry's Army friend. They had planned to go to Nashville, then north to meet at the Schmitt farm. But knowing they were being followed, those plans would not work because the authorities would be waiting.

Until the sheriff could come to get the man whose horse went lame, Jeremy and the other members of the posse had taken him to the village jail to be locked up in chains.

Sleep didn't come easily for William that night because too many questions ran through his thoughts. *Where were the Schmitts going? If they continued east, they would be heading away from Russellville. Would they double back and return to attack the farm again? Probably not. The Russells were on guard now. But if that were the Schmitts' plan, then there needed to be guards at least until Williams' father returned from Knoxville. There also needed to be men on the lookout for the Schmitts. That would be the sheriff's job. Someone had been sent to the county seat to get the sheriff. Nathan believed the sheriff would get to Russellville the next day.*

The Schmitts were fugitives now with a murder charge against them. They had been careless and left too much evidence of their involvement in the murders of Miron Adams and Jim. Plus, the man Lone Bear caught had identified Henry and Benjamin Schmitt as the killers.

Chapter Twenty-Five

Knoxville

The rain had continued most of the night. The men and women slept with their guns close--all except Lydia Russell, who did not like guns and didn't know how to shoot one.

The clouds were gone and bright sunshine lit the room as William awoke. Lone Bear and Jock were already up and in the kitchen drinking coffee. So were Mary and William's mother. Uncle Nathan and Aunt Lydia came down from one of the upstairs bedrooms a short time later. After breakfast they would hitch up their wagon and return to their home in Russellville to get ready for the funeral.

Word of the murders and the funeral plans had spread rapidly. People came from the farms that surrounded Russellville and from the village. They brought food for the Adams' family. Even the two, free black families that lived on small farms north of the Blue River came to support Betty, Jim's wife, whom they knew.

A circuit-riding preacher, from over by a new settlement caller Hillsdale, had been sent for to conduct the funeral service for Miron Adams and Jim.

The Preacher was eloquent with his eulogy. He directed the people who were gathered in the singing of several hymns. The prayers were long and full of Bible quotations. Nathan Russell spoke about his friend, Miron, their time in the Army together, and their trek from Virginia to Russellville.

After the burial, William suggested that he and Lone Bear should try to pick up the two Schmitts' trail, and William's Uncle Nathan agreed. Jock felt he should stay at the farm with one of the men from town in case the farm was the Schmitt's target. Mary looked relieved. She liked Jock and knew he would protect her, her mother, and her brothers. William knew that Jock really wanted to go with Lone Bear and him, but Jock would be of better use at the farm. Besides Jock didn't ride horseback and trailing the Schmitts would require riding a horse.

William and Lone Bear headed for the last place Henry and Benjamin Schmitt were known to be. They would try to pick up the Schmitt's trail. This plan might be a waste of time because of the rain. If they could not find the trail, instead, they would go to Knoxville to catch William's father before he started back to Russellville with the freight wagons. They needed to warn him that the Schmitts were hunting him and had killed Miron Adams and Jim.

William and Lone Bear found the deadfall where the note had been left and the brook where the trail had been lost. They searched downstream for two hours and found nothing. The rain had done its job and washed all signs away. The two started for Knoxville and William's father.

Trying to figure out the murderers' strategy was on William's mind. He believed that the Schmitts knew his father was in Knoxville and that they planned to ambush him on the road, probably somewhere between Maryville and Russellville, but where? He wondered. *With the*

Schmitts in front of them and waiting somewhere along the road, William decided they should take a northern route to Knoxville and avoid the road all together. He did not want to ride into the Schmitts' trap. They knew William would be trailing them, and, probably, he would not be alone, so they would be watching the road in both directions.

It was over 60 miles to Knoxville, and the trail Lone Bear and he were taking would add several miles to the trip because it went north crossing the Holston River. Their journey would take two days to get there.

They entered Knoxville by taking the ferryboat, a wooden barge tethered on a cable that was stretched from the Knoxville side of the river to the opposite bank. Two men on the barge pulling on the cable propelled it across the river.

Once in Knoxville, Lone Bear said he would look around the city for the Schmitts, and check the stables for the Schmitts' horses. The Schmitts would not bother him because Benjamin Schmitt would not know him, and Henry Schmitt might not recognize him, or even if Henry did recognize him, he probably would not make the Russell connection.

William went straight to the hotel where his father was staying and found him in his room working on some legal documents that were to be filed with the land office.

William told his father of the murders and that the Schmitts were now hunting him. The news of his friend's murder and the murder of his loyal helper, Jim, hit William Sr. hard. However, grieving would have to wait. The Schmitts might even now be in Knoxville stalking him. William and his father were going to need some help looking for the Schmitts.

The two men began working out a plan to learn if the Schmitts were in Knoxville or if they had been there. William's father went to the bar next to the hotel lobby to see if any of his brother, Nathan's freight wagon drivers were having a drink. While his father went looking for the freighters, William took the opportunity to study the large, square opposite the hotel.

This Town Square, with its green grass and trees, was near the center of the city, and it had many benches for people to sit on. Quite a few of the town's people were taking advantage of the mild, spring weather and the Square's pleasant surroundings.

Just out of eyeshot, William stood to the side of the window so anyone looking up from the street or the Square could not see him. However, from his vantage point, he could observe both the street and the Square. As his eyes adjusted to the gloom of approaching night, he noticed Lone Bear sitting next to one of the trees in the Square watching the parade of people pass.

By the time his father returned to the hotel room with two of the wagon drivers, William had seen nothing of note. The men turned their attention to making a plan to gather information.

Benjamin Schmitt was well known in Knoxville. If he was there, he might be easy to find. Henry would be less known and harder to locate. Also, William Sr. had learned from a deputy in the bar that the authorities in Knoxville had been notified of the murders in Russellville.

Since William Sr. knew the county sheriff personally, he volunteered to make that contact. William didn't believe the Schmitts would try anything with so many people out and about. Knoxville was the State Capital; this city's prominence made it a busy town with activity on every street. It even had a small police force to handle the rowdy elements of its population and to solve the occasional crimes. The police were aware of the recent crimes, so they would be on the lookout for the Schmitts, too.

The two teamsters would visit the taverns and saloons of Knoxville to try and pick up information on the Schmitts. Saloons are full of talkative people, and some discreet questions about the Schmitts might turn up their whereabouts. William would accompany one of the teamsters, a capable Irishman named Michael Boyle. The other teamster, Sean Hennessy, would search alone. They all planned to meet back at the hotel in two hours.

William went to the window and signaled Lone Bear to come to his father's hotel room to fill the Indian in on the plan and to learn if he had found out anything.

Lone Bear was introduced to the teamsters. If the Schmitts were in the city, he had not found them.

The men left the room separately so they could not be connected as a group. Each went about his assigned task.

Two hours later they gathered again in the hotel room. William's father arrived first, followed by Sean Hennessy, then Lone Bear, and last William and Michael Boyle slipped in.

The sheriff had received a report about the murders in Russellville, but he did not know that the Schmitts might be in Knoxville. Immediately, deputies were called in and briefed on the murders and that the killers might be in the area. The Knoxville police were also notified. The law was now looking for the Schmitts.

Sean Hennessy had talked to a bartender who had seen Benjamin Schmitt that very morning in a tavern down by the river. He had been asking about William Russell Sr. and about when the freight wagons would be leaving for Russellville. The bartender said that Henry was not with him.

Lone Bear had found a campsite off the road to Maryville. The hoof tracks were those of the Schmitt's horses. The cut-boot print was all over the camp site. The Schmitts had been there the previous night but had abandoned it early in the morning. Sean volunteered to inform the sheriff of their findings.

The freight wagons were loaded and ready to start the return trip to Russellville early the next morning. William and his father decided to stick around the hotel that night and not take chances. Lone Bear was uncomfortable in the hotel and said he would be back in the morning. The teamsters left to join some of their fellows for a final night out.

At sunup the next morning the freight wagons were moving, each drawn by a team of four mules. There were eight extra mules (tethered in twos behind the wagons) brought along to be used as replacements should anything happen to the mules pulling the wagons. There were two outriders on horses to help keep the wagons rolling. Outriders came in handy when fording rivers. Each man was armed with a rifle, a pistol, and a knife. Carrying their rifles across their saddles, William and his father rode at the front of the mule train.

There probably would not be any trouble until they passed Maryville, but the Schmitts were unpredictable so everyone rode wary.

When Lone Bear rode up to the wagon train, Maryville was a mile behind them. As William had figured, Lone Bear had been scouting the road ahead of them. He found no trace of the Schmitts for the next five miles. That didn't surprise William Sr. because the area around Maryville was heavily populated. With farms on both sides of the road, this area was not a good place for an ambush--too many people around, and the ambushers might be seen.

William had been thinking about places on the road that the Schmitts might use to their advantage. *For example, the stretch of road that followed a creek meandering its way through the foothills of the Great Smoky Mountains might be a likely spot for an ambush. From the top of one of those hills that overlooked the road, the range for a shot would be one-hundred-to-one-hundred-and-fifty feet. A man with a long rifle could make that shot easily.*

The wagon train camped that night in a meadow not far from the road. This spot was a favorite camping place for the freighters and settlers moving into Tennessee. The meadow had plenty of fresh grass for the animals. The wagons were parked in a loose circle with the hobbled animals close by. The Cherokee were known to sneak into an unprepared camp and steal anything they could get their hands on, particularly horses. This area was the hunting grounds for the Cherokee, and they were not happy about white men being there. This land belonged to the Cherokee and white men were on it.

William Sr. posted two guards. They would be relieved every three hours. Everyone would take a turn as a guard. Walking around would help keep those on guard duty awake. The camp fire was in the center of the circle of wagons. No one looked directly into the fire because eyes do not adjust quickly if they have been staring into a fire. The posted guards looked into the dark and listened to the night sounds. This kind of vigilance would help keep them safe through the night.

As they sat around the campfire that night, William explained his thinking to his father, Lone Bear, and Michael Boyle. They agreed that the isolated stretch of road William remembered would be a good spot for an ambush. There were no farms around, and escape to the north would be easy. To the south were the Smoky Mountains with few trails and difficult passes. The Schmitts were lazy and less likely to go into the mountains. The flat lands with their thick forests and rivers where they lived would probably be their choice for an escape.

But both sides of the road needed to be scouted. The time had come for the hunted to become the hunters.

Gene House

William would scout the northern side, and Lone Bear would scout the southern side. If the Schmitts were spotted, whoever found them would return to the train and get help. The scouts' horses would remain with the train. Both men preferred to be on foot when moving through the dense forest. Horses make noise which might give their presence away.

William Sr. would stay with the wagon train and make himself a poor target by constantly riding around the wagons. After all, he was expected to be with the train. The Schmitts might not know of William and Lone Bear's presence with the train. Michael Boyle would drive the first wagon and keep a close watch. Having dodged the British in Ireland before coming to America, Michael had good training for this sort of maneuver.

Chapter Twenty-Six

Ambush by the Road

Before dawn William and Lone Bear slipped out of camp. The previous night they had selected several bird calls to use as signals. The Yellow Bellied Sap Sucker's whistles were chosen because very few of those birds lived in Eastern Tennessee. To use the calls of a bird common to Eastern Tennessee might get confusing, particularly if a real bird started answering their calls.

William knew his father didn't like having him searching for men who would kill him given half-a-chance, but William Sr. had accepted the plan as the best way. He had taught all of his sons everything he knew about tracking, hunting, fighting, and self-defense. In spite of his youth, William had proved to be very capable in each of these skills. William's father had often said, "William is the best tracker in the family."

When the Schmitts were located, William had promised to bring his father into the hunt. They would try to take the Schmitts alive to hold for trial, but knowing the Schmitts, this live capture might be impossible.

Gene House

William went deep into the forest, circled back toward the road, crossed game trails, and examined each trail for signs of men or horses passing. He found no sign. There were a few farms in the area, and he stopped at each to inquire about two riders. At the last farm before the stretch of road where he suspected an ambush might take place, the farmer said he had seen two riders pass the previous day. But he did not know who they were, and they did not stop.

From that farm for the next seven or eight miles, there were no farms, and no one lived near the road. It was a very isolated stretch. If the Schmitts had passed this farm yesterday and if they planned their ambush for this secluded section, then their night camp had to be some place far away from the road. It occurred to William that there might be hoof prints in the road dirt to identify the riders who passed the farm. Going to the road to look for Schmitt signs might be dangerous if they were watching. William slipped back into the forest. When he felt sure he had retreated far enough to be out of sight of anyone watching the road from the north side, William made the Sap-Sucker call and received an answering call from the other side of the road. Lone Bear was not far away.

As William waited near the road, he listened to the sounds of the forest for anything out of the ordinary. Nothing unusual. Silently, Lone Bear came and stood beside him. A quick description of what the farmer had told him, and Lone Bear was in the road looking for any track signs. William remained hidden. In a few minutes Lone Bear came back. The Schmitts' tracks were in the road but about a day old. No attempt had been made to hide them. *Why?* William pondered. *Were the Schmitts so sure no one was following them? Were they careless? They were fugitives who were not concealing themselves. Maybe they were being very shrewd. Maybe they knew Lone Bear and he were after them. "Do not under*

188

estimate the Schmitts," his father had warned. *"That old man is cagy. He is capable of anything. Be very careful."*

Lone Bear went back to the road, and staying in the shadows beside the road, he followed the Schmitts' trail. William moved deeper into the forest. About two miles farther down the road, Lone Bear found where the Schmitts had left the road and gone south into the rolling hills. Instead of whistling a signal, he found William. They decided to backtrack far enough so that they could not be seen, and both men then crossed the road.

Spreading out deep in the forest, the two men searched for any signs of the Schmitts. William found a hoof print with the crossed-shoe on a small game trail leading south into a little valley. Staying high on the hillside and in the shadows of the trees, they moved into the valley. A hundred yards into the valley, they found the Schmitts' campsite concealed by the trees. The Schmitts' horses were there, but the men were not. Quietly, William and Lone Bear backed away. While Lone Bear stayed and watched, William went for his father.

When William reached the wagon train, it was in front of the farm where the Schmitts had been seen riding past the previous day. This area was about a-half-mile before the road entered the isolated section. The train had stopped to water the stock at a small stream beside the road.

William Sr. had changed into buckskins and moccasins. His frock coat, breeches and shoes were packed away.

"I'm going with you to capture the Schmitts," his father stated.

Michael Boyle would take the train down the road, and one of the outriders would ride point. William Sr. charged Michael with getting the wagons through to Russellville. To give the Russell men time to find Lone Bear and to make a plan for capturing the Schmitts,

Michael would not start the wagon train down the road for a-half-hour.

Both Michael Boyle and Sean Hennessey wanted to join the Russells in the search for the Schmitts, but William's father thought they should stay with the wagon train and guard it. Reluctantly, they agreed. The two Irishmen loved a good fight, and they did not like being left out of this one.

With the train moving down the center of the road and no Russell to be seen, the Schmitts might be confused enough for the Russells and Lone Bear to get the drop on them. The wagon train would be the diversion to keep the Schmitts' attention.

William and his father moved quietly through the forest to the place where they were supposed to meet Lone Bear. He was not there. They waited and a few minutes later, Lone Bear walked up beside them unseen or heard until he was two steps away.

"You are very good," William Sr. exclaimed.

Lone Bear accepted the compliment with a grunt. "Maybe I steal the Schmitts' horses," Lone Bear, suggested with a wary smile.

"That might be a good idea, but if one of them whinnied, it would warn the Schmitts," William Sr. said. "We should leave the horses where they are for now."

Lone Bear had located the Schmitts. He described their ambush site. They had selected a well-hidden spot in some pine trees and bushes on a hill overlooking the road. This site was within easy rifle range of the road. A meadow below them extended from the road to the base of the hill. The hill had rocks and brush covering the slope but no obstructions to their view. The whole train would be clearly visible when it came down the road.

Lone Bear led the Williams to a place where the Schmitts' ambush site could be seen but out of their sight. They were in a pocket protected on three sides. Directly behind their position a very steep rock face soared up above them and wrapped around to protect their left flank. On their other side, the hill gently sloped away with a thick stand of pine trees covering it.

Lone Bear pointed to a ledge on the rock face about twenty feet up. If someone could get up on that ledge and get behind the Schmitts, catching them would be a lot easier. However, climbing to that ledge without making noise might be difficult. Lone Bear thought he could do it, and William Sr. agreed.

William and his father decided their best approach would be to work their way up the hill through the pine trees. This would keep them to the Schmitts' right and as much behind them as possible.

After waiting enough time for Lone Bear to reach the ledge, they began moving up the hill. Quietly from tree-to-tree-to-bush, always advancing from cover-to-cover, the men made their way up the slope. They always left the cover from a different spot than the place where they had entered, and they always located their next cover two or three steps away. Step . . . step . . . dive for cover before someone watching could aim and fire. Once under cover they moved immediately. The Indians had perfected this method of advancing on an enemy.

William launched himself to the next tree with brush around it. As he dove behind the tree, a rifle shot bellowed, and the branch where his head had been, shattered into a hundred pieces. The Schmitts were waiting for them. Obviously, they knew the Russells were coming.

"Thought you could sneak up on us, did you? Guess we fooled you!" Someone snickered under his breath.

It was the old man. "We saw you yesterday, young fellow. Henry said you would be along with your father, and now here you are. We will finish this fight now."

"Benjamin Schmitt," William Sr. warned, "you are

outnumbered and without horses. Give up. You can't get away. My drivers have surrounded the hill. We won't hurt you. You will get a fair trial."

"You're bluffing. Your drivers are still with the wagon train. They won't come help you. You're all alone," Benjamin shouted. His voice did not match his words. He was unsure.

Where was Henry? Usually, he was very talkative, but he had said nothing, William thought. *Then he knew. Henry was sneaking around behind them.* Quickly, William turned just in time to catch a movement in the trees to his left. Without taking aim, he fired into the bushes next to the tree where he had seen the movement.

A stream of curses erupted from the bushes. "You shot me, you little cheater!"

Giving away his position, Benjamin yelled and moved toward his son. William Sr. fired, hitting the old man in the shoulder. The old man fired back at William Sr. The rifle ball hit the dirt directly in front of him, spattering dirt in his eyes, temporarily blinding him. Henry had recovered enough to get a shot at William. The rifle ball hit the tree where William had taken cover. He could see his father was having trouble getting the dirt out of his eyes. William looked toward where Benjamin Schmitt was hiding. The old man raised up pointing a pistol at William Sr. Two bullets hit Benjamin Schmitt almost at the same time. William had fired his pistol, hitting Benjamin in the midsection. Lone Bear had fired from the ledge, hitting him in the head. Benjamin Schmitt fell to the ground and didn't move. Life had left him.

"Henry, give up! Your father's dead. There is a rifle pointed at your head from the ledge and more men are coming. Toss out your weapons," William shouted.

A shout from below confirmed William's words as Michael Boyle and Sean Hennessy and two other teamsters climbed over the edge of the hill.

More curses and threats on the Russells' lives, as a rifle got pushed into view, followed by a pistol.

"The knife too, Henry," William ordered.

Henry threw his knife. It stuck in a tree a few feet from William.

"That could have gotten you killed, Henry, if Lone Bear had not seen where the knife would land," William mocked.

"Lone Bear? That Indian from the deer killing? Pa said he thought there was someone else with you," Henry muttered, as William walked over to him. Lone Bear came up behind Henry and moved his weapons out of reach. Henry's shoulder had been smashed by William's bullet. His arm hung useless at his side.

"You wait until my uncle and my brother hear about this. They will come for you," threatened Henry.

"I wouldn't count on them much. They are being chased out of the state by Federal Marshals," William replied.

Michael Boyle knelt beside William Sr. to wash his eyes out with some canteen water. The debris in his eyes was being stubborn. Also, his face had been cut in several places. These cuts were cleaned, too. Michael thought it would take a doctor to get all the dirt out of William Sr.'s eyes. The older Russell found it hard not to rub his eyes, but he listened to Michael who seemed to know what he was talking about when he said that rubbing the eyes could damage them further and make it more difficult to see again. "Keep your eyes closed. I will cover them with a bandage when we get back to the wagons and you can get to Russellville and the doctor," Michael instructed.

Henry cursed and complained about how much his shoulder hurt. Finally, as Henry was led down the hill to where the wagons waited, Michael had had enough. "If you don't be quiet, I'll hit you over the head and make you be quiet."

Henry was sullen but quiet for a while. Michael bandaged Henry's shoulder and put the arm in a sling.

Lone Bear brought the Schmitts' horses to where Benjamin Schmitt lay. Sean and Lone Bear loaded the body on one of the horses and took it to the wagons.

Not sure what to do next, the men gathered around William Sr. Both Henry and William Sr. needed a doctor. The closest one was in Russellville some twenty miles away.

William Sr. took over. Benjamin Schmitt needed to be buried. If the sheriff wanted the body, he could come dig it up. William and his father would ride to Russellville and the doctor. Riding hard, Russellville could be made in the few hours before the sun set. Henry would be bounced around a lot, but that couldn't be helped. Henry could choose to ride with them or to go the next day with the wagons. Henry wanted no part of a jolting horseback ride. He was in too much pain. He chose to stay with the wagons. Lone Bear would stay and guard him.

William saddled their horses, and they left immediately with William leading his father's horse. William Sr. was a good rider, but with his eyes bandaged, all he could do was hold on to the saddle and follow William.

The teamsters got shovels from one of the wagons and dug a grave. Benjamin was wrapped in his blanket and buried. Michael Boyle got a board from a wagon and wrote on it:

Here lies Benjamin Schmitt
Killed by revenge
May 17, 1815

This marker, Michael stuck into the ground at the head of the grave.

Sean gave Henry a big slug of whiskey for the pain. Henry said nothing as he watched his father being buried. One of the teamsters read from a Bible.

Shackles were put on Henry's ankles, and he was loaded into the back of one of the wagons. Lone Bear rode behind the wagon where he could watch Henry. With a crack of the whip over the horses' heads, Michael started the wagon train for Russellville.

Chapter Twenty-Seven

Race for Help

This late in May the days were longer than the nights, so the two Russells galloped down the main street of Russellville before the sun disappeared for the day. The doctor's cabin was at the very end of the street. They rode straight to it. William helped his father down. With his wife behind him holding a lamp, the doctor answered the pounding on the door. He ushered William Sr. into his examining room and asked his wife to light more lamps.

William Sr. explained what had happened and answered the doctor's questions as he removed the bandage. The doctor was in charge now. There was nothing William could do to help, so he went outside to look after the horses. They were good horses, but they had been used hard and needed attention.

Several men, including Jeremy Alexander, were waiting for William in front of the doctor's cabin. As he started to tell of the encounter with the Schmitts, his uncle Nathan ran up asking about his brother.

"Pa got some dirt and debris spattered in his face and

eyes by a Schmitt rifle ball. The doctor is examining him now," William told his uncle. Then, William told the story of the Schmitts setting a trap for the two Russell men. He described the brief fight on the hill where Benjamin Schmitt had been killed, how his father's eyes had been injured, and when Henry Schmitt had been shot and captured. Nathan listened to William tell of the fight then went into the doctor's cabin to see his brother.

The stable man was among those who stood in front of the doctor's cabin, listening. William asked him if he would stable their two horses for the night. The stable owner immediately agreed and led the tired horses toward his barn. William indicated he would be along in a few minutes to get their gear, and then he went inside to check on his father. The doctor had washed William Sr.'s eyes with a mild solution of herb water.

"The herb gives the water some sort of numbing ability to help relieve the feeling of having something in your eyes." The doctor informed the men. "I have washed all the dirt I can see out of the eyes. Also, I removed a piece of pine needle that had stuck in the blue of the retina."

The doctor rebandaged William Sr.'s eyes and strongly recommended that it would be best if he kept his eyes covered and didn't try to use them for a few days.

"The eyes needed time to heal themselves," the doctor explained. He gave William a stack of bandages and a small bottle of the eye wash to flush the eyes two-or-three times a day.

Followed by the doctor and his wife, William guided his father out into the cool, evening air. Nathan and Jeremy drove up in Nathan's wagon to drive the Williams to their farm.

A half-moon had risen in the dark sky by the time Nathan turned his wagon into the path leading to the Russells' front door. Jock heard the wagon coming and lit a torch in the front yard. Martha and Mary came out onto the porch to see who could be coming this late at night. When they saw William Sr. with his bandaged head, they rushed to him, asking questions faster than anyone could possibly answer.

"Now, Martha," William Sr. soothed. "I am going to be fine. I just got some dirt in my eyes, and as a precaution the doctor wants me to keep my eyes bandaged for a few days. He will be out to see me tomorrow or the next day. Don't you worry none," and he kissed his wife and hugged his daughter. The women helped him into the house.

William thanked his Uncle Nathan and Jeremy for driving them out to the farm. Satisfied that his brother would be all right, Nathan turned the wagon around and headed back to town.

Jock folded his arms around his rifle watching William and waiting for the details of the day's events. James came from the barn where he had waited until they knew who was driving up the lane. He wanted to hear the story, too. William recounted all that had happened.

When William finished, Jock huffed, "Let's hope the Schmitts have learned their lesson. Don't fight the Russells."

"Do you think Henry's trial will be in Russellville?" James asked.

"My father thinks the trial should be in Knoxville. If Henry is kept here, he's liable to get hung before there is a trial," answered William.

"Miron Adams was well-liked. Some people been talking about hanging the Schmitts as soon as they were caught. They are saying there is no need for a trial," James added.

"The United States is a country of laws where you're thought to be innocent until someone shows you are not. Not like England where you get accused, and right away the authorities think you're guilty," Jock reminded them.

He continued, "That is one of the reasons I want to live in this country. Tennessee is a state with laws against murder, but murder must be proven in a court of law before a man's life is taken from him. When a man dies, it is permanent. We should be very sure before we kill a man. A trial with a jury will make sure Henry is guilty before he gets hung."

"He's guilty," William said "but you're right, Jock, a judge and jury need to say so before he's hung."

The three friends went inside the house. William Sr. was sitting in his arm chair with a cup of coffee in his hand.

Martha Russell came into the room, asking, "William, are you hungry? Your father said you didn't stop to eat getting here, so I'm fixing him some eggs and bacon. Would you like some?"

"You bet I would," William replied, realizing how empty his insides felt. Better make mine at least a-half-dozen eggs and ten-or-twelve slices of bacon."

"Actually," he joked, "I am hungry enough to eat a whole cow. And, do you have any bread?"

"Well, the hens have been busy, so we have plenty of eggs although Jock eats enough for two men," she replied, teasing Jock and giving him a big smile.

Mary was standing beside her mother, and she gave Jock a big smile, too, but it was more than a tease.

When the food was ready, Martha led her husband to the table. The others joined them with cups of hot coffee all around. While William and his father ate, they discussed the day and the events leading up to it.

During William's absence, a Knoxville deputy sheriff had come for the man that Lone Bear and Nathan had caught after the raid on the farm. The deputy had told Nathan, as well, that the three other Schmitts had escaped into the Mississippi Territory with the Federal Marshals following them.

"You know I've wondered what it would be like to be blind," William Sr. observed, "but I never realized how many forks full of air one has to eat, before one gets the food into one's mouth," as some egg fell from his fork just as it reached his mouth.

Smiling, Martha helped her husband to finish his eggs. The bacon he had no problem with because he could pick that up with his hand.

The food had disappeared, including the last slice of bread which Jock devoured with a lot of butter and jam.

"I declare, Jock," Mary teased, "how can you eat after that big supper we fed you not more than an hour ago?"

Jock just grinned at her and patted his stomach.

William Sr., led by his wife, went upstairs to their room. William began to realize how tired he felt. He was ready for sleep and went upstairs to his bed. James, who was sleeping in the barn, excused himself and, carrying a lantern, went to the barn. He told Jock he would check on Blue Belle.

Mary and Jock sat in the front room in the candle-light, talking. They spent time talking whenever time permitted.

As William rested his head on the feather pillow, he thought about Mary and Jock. *What could they possibly find to talk about he had asked his mother? She had just smiled and said you should know. What did you and Maria talk about? That was different he had said. She talked about her dancing, and I told her about the farm. But a light clicked on in William's head. Jock might become his brother-in-law. He slipped off to sleep.*

The next day, late in the afternoon, the wagon train with its prisoner arrived. The doctor treated Henry Schmitt's wound, removing some buckskin and shirt fabric that Michael Boyle had not seen when he removed the rifle ball. The doctor put some kind of poultice on the wound to try to prevent infection. Then Henry was locked in the storage shed behind The Trading Post to wait for the sheriff.

The doctor had driven out to the farm earlier in the day. He had examined William Sr.'s eyes in daylight and could find no more dirt or debris in his eyes, but because William Sr. felt something, the doctor instructed Martha to keep his eyes bandaged between washings.

That evening, William Sr. had some good news for his family when Martha removed the bandage to wash his eyes. He said he could see light and blurred forms around him, but his eyes still felt as though they had dirt in them.

James returned to his family's farm to help with the chores.

Jock completed the work of getting the sulky ready for the trip to St. Louis. A padded seat that held two people comfortably had replaced the original make-shift-seat. Mary had helped with sewing the seat cushion. Under the seat Jock had constructed a large compartment to carry tools and equipment.

The next afternoon Jock and Mary went riding to try out the new, rebuilt sulky. Mary packed a basket lunch, and they drove to a clearing beside a fast-running brook about a mile from the farm for their picnic. Although nothing had been said, it was becoming obvious to everyone that there would be a wedding soon.

Jeremiah, William's older brother, returned home a few days after the Schmitt ambush. His arrival safe and sound had put the family in a celebration mood. Martha and Mary fixed his favorite dinner. After dinner everyone gathered on the front lawn under the big Oak, drinking coffee and swapping Army stories. Jeremiah could be a talker and excellent story teller. He held sway with tales of his experiences in the Army. The men agreed, no matter what unit of the Army one serves in, some things are always the same. The family had a shining time that night.

Chapter Twenty-Eight

Jock's New Home

Some of the neighbors and residents of Russellville had learned of Jock's carpentry skills and requested his help with projects they either could not do themselves or did not want to do. Jeremy Alexander wanted Jock to build two more rooms on the tavern to accommodate more travelers. Nathan needed more merchandise shelves for The Trading Post, and The Doctor wanted to improve his examination room. Jock was becoming very busy. He needed an area of his own where he could work. He felt he should move to town and build a shop and a house.

Jock purchased an acre of land near the doctor's cabin from Nathan Russell and began construction of a small house. Mary helped Jock with its design. It would be a two-story, frame house with two bedrooms upstairs and a kitchen and main room with fireplace on the first floor. A covered porch would be built across its front. The foundation would be constructed with the same native stone used for the fireplace. Jock hired a stone mason, who had recently moved to Russellville, to help. The lumber for the floor and the house was easier to get now than when Nathan had started the frame house for his wife. A saw mill had been built by two brothers about two miles from town on a small creek, thus providing a continual supply of cut wood.

Jock's barn would have two stalls, a large work area, and storage for grain and hay for Blue Belle.

James and William helped Jock dig a well where the kitchen would be. Jock used the sulky to haul the foundation stones from a rocky ledge not too far from the village. When the foundations were ready and the lumber all delivered and stacked, the date for the raising was set. The residents of Russellville came from all around to help Jock raise his barn and house. A raising was a celebration of the community helping a neighbor.

The men brought their tools, and the women fixed a large lunch for everyone. The children played games and enjoyed the outing. The older boys helped where they could and were taught building construction. In one day the barn was raised with sides and roof completed. Jock had finished the framing of the house, so the siding and roof went up quickly. The work was finished by mid-afternoon. With many thanks from Jock, people packed up their gear and headed home. The interior finishing work would be Jock's to do, of course, but he now had a house and barn of his own.

"Many lonely nights on Lafitte's ships when I stood watch, I thought about having a home of my own," Jock told his friends. "In those days, I never expected it to happen. Now, I have friends who don't care that once I was a pirate."

People on the frontier accepted a man for how he conducted himself. They did not judge a man on what he once had been or had done. The Russells had welcomed him into their family without question, and he was in love with their daughter. They would be married in the fall . . .

if William Sr. gave his consent. But first, Jock would go with William to St. Louis to see Maria Olivarez and fulfill the promise they had made to Miss Olivia.

Two deputy sheriffs came and took Henry Schmitt to Knoxville. His trial was scheduled for the following week. The residents of Russellville speculated as to whether Henry would live to be tried. His wound had gotten infected because he kept pulling the poultices off when they started itching. The doctor said the itching was a sign the wound had started to heal. Henry just leveled a stream of curses at the doctor, the sheriff, and particularly the Russells. He blamed everyone but himself for his troubles.

The days grew warmer. The never-ending work on the farm kept everyone busy. William labored from sun up to sunset trying to do his father's work, as well as, his own. But his impatience to leave for St Louis grew. As soon as his father's eyes were working again, William would leave.

William Sr.'s eyes were healing with no complications. The doctor credited the recovery to both Martha and William Sr. for obeying his instructions.

The day of Henry Schmitt's trial arrived. Henry's infection had been checked. The doctor in the county seat had used an Indian cure to slow the spread of the infection so Henry could stand trial. Lone Bear came from his village in the western Mississippi Territory. The Russell men with James, Jock, and Jeremy Alexander rode to the county seat to testify.

The trial lasted two days. Each of the men were witnesses for the prosecution. The defense called several neighbors of the Schmitts who testified they had seen the Schmitts elsewhere on the day of Miron Adams' murder. In the end the jury found Henry guilty, but because there was no eye witness to the murders, the judge sentenced Henry to thirty years at hard labor in the Tennessee State

Prison system. The Adams' family was upset that Henry had not been sentenced to hang.

As soon as the trial ended, Lone Bear left for his village. Some white families had homesteaded on the Indians' tribal land. A number of the young warriors were talking about driving them off. The land was the Choctaws by treaty, and as a leader of his people, he was needed there. William Sr. told Lone Bear that he and his family would always be welcome in Russellville. William offered to help in whatever ways he could. James and Jock echoed these sentiments. The white men knew that the Indians were being forced from their ancestral lands. Nothing was going to stop the western migration of the land-hungry, white men. Maybe, Lone Bear knew this too, but he said nothing.

Chapter Twenty-Nine

Rachel Jackson

William's plans to begin the trip to St. Louis and Maria had been delayed by the Schmitts' attack, his father's injury, and Henry's trial. Now, there was nothing more to keep him at the farm. His father's eyes were fully recovered. The crops were growing in the fields. The trees and bushes were leafed in their new, green splendor. The Narcissuses had bloomed and died as the Tulips replaced them pushing their beautiful, red blossoms into the air. The Irises were growing around the garden. Soon, they would bloom. The Tiger Lilies were growing like weeds. Summer would be here soon.

The date for William to begin the trip to St. Louis had been set the day William Sr. announced he could see without a problem. Jock and James would accompany William. They both had met Maria on that memorable day in New Orleans. Jock had met her mother, Miss Olivia, and had promised her that he would go to St. Louis to help William find Maria.

Jock's rebuilt sulky would make the trip more

comfortable for all. The cargo box under the seat was large enough to carry most of the gear they would need for the trip. There was even enough room for a large canvas tarpaulin to use as a shelter from the rain. William and James rode their horses while Jock drove the sulky, with Blue Belle proudly trotting in front.

Jeremiah listened to his younger brother as he talked about Maria Olivarez and the promise made to her mother. Jeremiah had been asked by some of his Army friends to join them in an expedition up the Missouri River to explore the land that would be the Bounty Land given to the veterans of the 1812 War. He had told them he would join the expedition, but first he needed to go home for a while to see his family. The veterans planned to meet north of St. Louis and build dugout canoes for the trip. William's planned trip to St. Louis was perfect for Jeremiah. He decided to join William then continue on to link up with the veteran's expedition.

The day finally came to begin the trip to St. Louis. William's excitement was high. He had been anticipating this day for weeks. He was up before dawn, packing his gear and saddling the stallion. When his mother called him for breakfast, he could hardly eat he was in such a state of anticipation. Jock had driven out from town the night before to see Mary and to be ready to leave in the morning. Jeremiah was up early also and ready to go. James would join them when they passed the Woods' farm.

After Jock's long goodbye to Mary, promising to return as soon as William had helped Maria break free of her brother's control, they set out for St. Louis. Mary extracted a promise from William to take care of Jock and bring him safely back to her. William promised he would, but it would probably be Jock who took care of him. The whole family stood in the yard and waved goodbye as the three men rode down the path to the road and turned toward the Woods' farm.

At the Woods' farm James was ready and waiting. Martha Woods came straight to William as he dismounted to greet the Woods' family. She took his hand and led him a short distance from the others.

"William," she said, "James has told me about this Spanish girl you are going to help. I know your interest is more than friendship. You must go and find this girl and talk with her to learn her interest in you. Please know that my interest in you is more than friendship. You need to know this and understand that I will be waiting for you. I will pray for your safe return home."

A lump rose quickly in William's throat. He had known Martha liked him as a friend, and he liked her. She was a beautiful young girl; no, she was a beautiful young woman. But he had not thought of her as more than a friend. Now, he understood she loved him.

"Martha, I . . .," he stammered.

Martha put her fingers on his lips saying, "don't say anything. You don't need to. We will talk when you return." She led him back to the others. There were hugs and "Goodbyes" all around. The four men rode out of the farm yard and disappeared down the road.

The four rode in silence for some time, each deep in his own thoughts.

William was recovering from Martha Woods' pronouncement about her feelings for him. *This confession had been unexpected. They had many things in common. Both liked farm life. She was good with animals and had several pets. He remembered how happy she had been showing him the lambs she had helped her father deliver. She always helped her father when the farm animals were giving birth. She also was good at nursing animals back to health when they got sick.*

Suddenly, it hit him. He was very attracted to her, also, he pondered. *And she was beautiful; her beauty attracted him on the physical level. He had much to think about now. She knew about Maria. What had James told her? He would ask James that tonight.*

The men moved at a ground-eating trot so they could get as far each day as possible. They took care, though, not to wear out the horses on the first day. The trip would take about three weeks. William hoped they would reach St. Louis before the Fourth of July.

The men had planned their trip to proceed through the Cumberland Mountains, using one of the more northern passes. This route would take them to Nashville where they could replenish their supplies as needed. The road they chose went near The Hermitage, General Andrew Jackson's home outside of Nashville. Because all four men had served under "Old Hickory," they decided to take the General at his word and stop at The Hermitage to say "hello." The General had mentioned more than once to his troops that, if they ever came by his home, they were to stop, say "howdy," get some water, and maybe a bite to eat.

As they rode up The Hermitage carriage path to the house, they could see two black men working in a large garden to the east of the two-story, log blockhouse. It had been originally built for defense against Indians.

Upon seeing the approaching riders, one of the men went to the front door of the house and announced something to whoever was inside. A modestly dressed woman came out of the front door and stood on the porch waiting for the riders to arrive. She held a corncob pipe in one hand. As she waited, she took a puff from the pipe and blew out a large cloud of blue-gray smoke. Mrs. Rachel Jackson was an impressive woman, not beautiful, although for age and stress over her failed marriage to Colonel Lewis Robards, had worn on her. Then, the difficulty with legitimizing her marriage to Andrew Jackson had also taken its toll on her appearance. In spite of her hardships, there was obvious intelligence in her eyes.

The men came to a stop in front of Mrs. Jackson. Before dismounting they introduced themselves and explained that they had been in the Army serving under General Jackson. They were stopping to pay their respects to the General, and then they planned to continue on to Nashville before nightfall.

When Mrs. Jackson heard the name Russell, she asked if William and Jeremiah were kin to Major Jacob Russell. Upon learning that she was talking to two of his younger brothers, she invited the men to dismount and join her on the porch. Turning to the black man who had remained close by, she ordered him to water their horses. She explained that "the General wasn't at home today. He was off in Nashville on some kind of government business and would not return until later in the afternoon."

William asked, "You said Jacob is a Major now? The last time I saw him was in New Orleans after the battle, and he was a Captain then."

"Well, he got a promotion not too long ago and is commanding a battalion over in the Missouri Territory putting down some Indian trouble," she replied. "Excuse me, gentlemen. I'll be right back," and she entered the house.

In a few minutes she returned, followed by a young, black girl carrying a tray with slices of bread, butter, and meat. Another girl emerged from the house with a large pitcher of water and four tin cups which she poured the water into and handed to the men. The first girl proceeded to make sandwiches from the bread and meat with generous spreads of butter on the bread. These she handed to the men. The meat was cold, roasted beef.

Mrs. Jackson said that she couldn't send the brothers of one of her favorite officers away without something to eat and drink. She apologized for the poor fare, but it was

211

all she had on hand that day.

The men were grateful for the lunch.

"The General would never forgive me if I sent you away hungry," she teased, a twinkle in her eye demonstrating her famous wit.

Happy they stopped at The Hermitage and with full bellies, the men turned toward Nashville a few miles away. Built on the banks of the Cumberland River by the early settlers, the old blockhouse fort was still in use as the military headquarters. This headquarters would be where they would find General Jackson and get further news of their brother Jacob.

William and Jeremiah entered the headquarters' building and learned from the Sergeant on duty that the General had been called to the Kentucky boarder and was not expected for several days. Upon inquiring about Major Jacob Russell, the brothers were told that he had been given an assignment in the Missouri Territory putting down an Indian uprising. William asked the Sergeant if dispatches were being sent to the Major. The Sergeant allowed that a dispatch was being prepared to go to the Major the next day. William asked if his brother and he could include a letter to the major to inform him of their trip to St. Louis and the expedition up the Missouri River. The Sergeant said that the dispatch case was light and a one-or-two-page letter would be alright to include. The brothers quickly wrote a letter to their older brother and sealed it with the Sergeant's sealing wax.

Outside of the fort William and Jeremiah turned toward where James and the horses waited across the road in front of a store. Jock was coming out of the store with some supplies to replenish those they had consumed. As William looked back toward the old fort, a rider emerged from behind the fort not more than one-hundred-and-fifty-feet away. The rider was Henry Schmitt. Their eyes met in recognition. Instantly, Henry wheeled his horse and disappeared behind the fort at a dead run.

"It's Henry Schmitt," William shouted, as he ran to the sulky to retrieve his rifle. He leapt onto the chestnut, stallion's saddle and took off for the corner of the fort where Henry had disappeared. Turning the corner of the fort, he saw Henry just as he rounded a bend in the road and could no longer be seen. Plunging ahead at full gallop, William chased after Henry. William could hear James and Jeremiah following him. But as he turned the bend in the road where Henry had gone, the road was empty. Henry had left the road, but where? William slowed the big stallion to a walk and James and Jeremiah slowed their horses as they drew abreast of him.

"Are you certain that you saw Henry Schmitt, William?" James asked.

"Yes and he saw me, too," William breathed, a little winded from the sudden exertion.

"Well, if Henry has escaped from jail, he probably had some help, so he's not alone. If we try to follow him into the woods, we could be riding into an ambush. Maybe, we had better get the law involved," Jeremiah suggested.

"Jock went to find the sheriff when we left," James added. "Henry is their job, not ours. I think we should go back and tell the sheriff all we know."

"I agree with James," Jeremiah stated. "I know you want to catch Henry, William, and so do I, but he is the sheriff's problem now."

Very reluctantly, William agreed. He could track Henry, but it would help if the law rode with him. They turned back toward Nashville to find Jock and the sheriff.

Standing next to the sulky talking with Jock as the trio rode up, was a man with an official-looking badge on his shirt. Jock introduced him as a deputy sheriff. William explained about seeing Henry Schmitt, chasing him, and his escaping into the woods.

"Did any of you men," indicating the other two, "see this Henry Schmitt?" the deputy asked.

"It looked like Henry," James said. "He was turning and running when I looked, so I only got a glimpse. But if William says it was Henry, you can bet your last dollar on it being Henry."

"We haven't received notice of an escape from jail by any Henry Schmitt," the deputy said. "The sheriff is away on official business and is not expected to return until tomorrow. There are only two of us deputies for the whole county right now, so I can't leave without more proof of this Henry Schmitt's escape and sighting. Plus, I don't know you men, and I can't go chasing around after someone on just your say so."

William suppressed his anger, "Henry Schmitt is a convicted murderer and sentenced to thirty years in prison by the court in Knoxville. Since you don't know Henry, we will go with you to track him, identify him, and help you catch him."

"Well, I can't leave the city until the sheriff returns, so tracking this Schmitt person will have to wait for the sheriff to decide," the deputy said, obviously reluctant to pursue Henry Schmitt. "You men better wait around until tomorrow and talk to the sheriff."

"By tomorrow Henry Schmitt will be miles from here. He was going east when last we saw him, but he could go anywhere from here. If he's not known around Nashville, he could walk right by you, and you would never recognize him," William gritted his teeth, irritation showing. "You are losing your opportunity to catch a criminal. I don't think we will stay in Nashville any longer. We are taking the Natchez Trace south to buy horses. We have a time deadline, so we need to keep moving."

"But, William," Jeremiah said, starting to protest . . .

"OUCH! Jock, you stepped on my foot . . . ."

Jock had turned toward Jeremiah just as he started to speak.

"I'm sorry, Jeremiah, I didn't see you there. Blue Belle looks like she's getting restless. We better see about our horses. Come on," Jock said as he, with Jeremiah in tow, walked toward the horses.

"I think you men should stay in Nashville until the sheriff gets back," the deputy said, watching Jock and Jeremiah walk away.

"Sorry, deputy," William said. "Henry Schmitt has gone, and I don't think he will return. We only stopped in Nashville to pay our respects to General Jackson. He is a friend of the family. We served under him in the War. Now, we must be on our way."

"I could order you to stay, Mr. Russell," the deputy said with an edge in his voice. But the mention of General Jackson as a friend slowed him down some.

"Yes, you could," William agreed mildly. "But then you would have to pay for our hotel, for our meals, and for a stable and feed for our horses. You do that, and we'll stay right here in Nashville."

"We don't pay for hotels and meals," the deputy stammered loudly, his frustration showing. "You stay at your own expense."

"No, we're not going to do that," William replied, starting to walk toward the others. "By the way, what is your full name, deputy?"

"What do you want to know for?"

"Because when I write about seeing Henry Schmitt for the Knoxville newspaper, I want to get your name right," William replied.

"You a newspaper fellow?" the deputy asked.

"I write for them when a good story comes along," William lied.

"My name is Hinric Rinehart," the deputy replied.

William turned to face the deputy. "Henry Schmitt's

mother's maiden name was Rinehart; you're Henry's cousin! You're protecting a convicted murderer." William had noticed several people standing nearby listening to the conversation. Then, he saw eyes widen, and a woman, watching from a store doorway, gasped.

"Mister, his uncle is the sheriff, and if that murderer is around here, they are protecting him," one of the listening men commented loudly. "If I were you, I'd get out of here while the gettin's good."

"Thanks for the advice," William responded, watching the deputy.

The deputy's face was distorted with rage. His hand went to the butt of the pistol in his belt.

"You pull that pistol, and my brother will drop you where you stand. He is the best shot in our county. He won't miss," William said softly, but with the hard edge of conviction that left no doubt he spoke the truth.

The deputy glanced toward the men standing beside their horses. All three men held rifles ready. He moved his hand from the pistol butt.

"You won't get away with this. I order you to stay in Nashville. You're violating my order."

"We have broken no laws. We identified an escaped convict and tried to catch him for you. You, on the other hand, are shielding the convicted murderer, and you are helping him to escape. You have broken the law. I believe these nice people now know the truth about you and your uncle," William gestured, referring to the small crowd standing on the sidewalk, listening.

"When we have finished our business, I will return and catch Henry to return him to prison." William concluded.

William turned to see the Sergeant from the fort and several soldiers standing a few feet away. William walked directly to him: "Did you hear my exchange with the deputy?"

216

"We heard. I never did like that deputy," the Sergeant replied. "I will write a full report for General Jackson. He was the prosecutor for this county. He will know what you should do under these circumstances."

"We will return when our business is complete," William said. Then he mounted his horse, and the four rode out of Nashville south toward the Natchez Trace.

Wanting to put as many miles between them and the Rineharts and Schmitts as they could, the men rode south until well after dark. Jeremiah rode beside William along the narrow road.

"What tipped you that the deputy might be helping Henry Schmitt?" Jeremiah asked.

"First, although we were not introduced and we have never met before, he knew my name. Second, he was too reluctant to go after Henry. Third, he didn't want us tracking Henry. Fourth, he was not interested in a description of a criminal he professed not to know. And fifth, the name Hinric Rinehart was tooled into the leather of his belt. I remembered at Henry's trial his mother's maiden name of Rinehart being mentioned."

"You are observant, little brother," Jeremiah declared with affection. "I hope they don't learn where we are really going."

"I don't think we can count on that," William replied. "We must take precautions and be very careful. I will write to our father to alert him of Henry's escape."

Following an uneventful, cold camp that night, the men took the first trail that headed in a westerly direction. The trail was not made for a sulky. Several places it had to be carried around obstacles. They turned northwest, crossed the Cumberland River into Kentucky then crossed the Ohio River into Illinois. A-week-and-a-half later, without hearing or seeing anymore of the Schmitts and their kin, the men arrived in the small East St. Louis River port across the Mississippi River from St. Louis.

Chapter Thirty

Blackburn Hotel

The flat-bottomed ferry slowly approached the St. Louis landing, called "The Levee." The morning sun created eerie shadows on the unhurried current as the water sloshed under the boat. These shadows plus the rolling motion of the deck beneath their feet sometimes disturbed the horses. Each man stayed beside his horse to keep it calm. William tied a bandana over the big stallion's eyes to keep him from getting jumpy.

The Levee, a large, flat-rock, shelf about 100 yards deep and just as long, gently sloped into the river and provided a natural landing for all manner of boats. The shelf extended from the river's edge to the foot of a natural limestone bluff. The bluff rose forty feet above the levee. St. Louis had been built on top of the bluff. Roads leading from the levee to the city had been dug into the bluff at both ends.

In the summer of 1815, St. Louis was a thriving and fast-growing city. Trappers and fur traders got their supplies here before starting up the Missouri River in their keelboats. Merchants were bringing in goods for sale. Land speculators and settlers bound for the cheap land of the Missouri Territory outfitted here as they prepared to move to the frontier and stake their claims.

The Levee bustled with early morning activity. The four men watched the goings-on with interest as the ferry maneuvered into its landing space. Boats were being loaded and others were being unloaded. Teams of mules hitched to wagons were all over the Levee in a haphazard kaleidoscope of ever-changing action. Everywhere they looked something was happening. A steamboat anchored in the river appeared to be unloading large barrels into a flat-bottomed boat to be brought ashore.

Before the men had gone ten feet from the ferry, two hawkers, selling land and supplies for a trip up the Missouri, had tried to button-hole them. William led the way to the south road and followed a loaded wagon headed for the city. At the base of the road, Jock climbed onto the sulky's seat while William, James, and Jeremiah mounted. They rode up the hill and onto First Street.

"The plan is to split up and spread out over the city to learn about Fernando Hernandez and Manuel Olivarez without arousing anyone's curiosity. Maria should not be mentioned," William reminded them. "Let's pick a place where we can meet, say about noon. That will give us about three hours to learn what we can. I'll find Jacob to let him know we are here."

"When we rode up the hill, I could see some grass and shade at the south end of Second Street. That map of St. Louis the boatman showed us had only three streets west of the levee. It should be easy to find," James suggested.

"That's good with me," replied Jock. Jeremiah shook his head in agreement.

Shortly after noon the men had reunited in the shade

of a large Elm tree on the south edge of town; they were eating dried meat and some fresh fruit that Jeremiah had found. Their horses grazed nearby. Here they shared the information they had gathered.

Jeremiah's fellow veterans were hard at work building the dugout canoes. About half of their expected number had arrived. Jeremiah planned to join them after William's business with Maria got settled. He had also found out that Fernando Hernandez owned and operated a trading company on Second Street and that another Spanish man named Manuel Garcia was working with him. He had learned nothing about Maria.

Jock confirmed Jeremiah's information about the Hernandez Trading Company. He had also seen two men, identified as Fernando and Manuel, come out of the trading company offices, and they proceeded to a restaurant. By talking with some men loading a wagon for the company, Jock had learned the company was up for sale because the owner wished to be free for other pursuits. The men loading the wagon did not like their boss and were free with their talk.

Fernando had recently fought a duel on Bloody Island, a low brush and scrub-tree filled sandbar-island across the river from the city. The ferrymen had pointed it out when they crossed the river earlier. Fernando had wounded his opponent seriously. The man would recover, but as a result he would be in poor health for the rest of his life. The loading men had heard Manuel laughing about the poor man's marksmanship. He had shot too quickly, missing Fernando by several feet. Fernando had aimed at the man's arm wanting only to wound him. The wound would have been slight, but the man moved just as Fernando fired, and he was hit in the chest--a much more serious wound. This confirmed Fernando, the duelist, as a deadly pistol shot.

James had located the hotel, really more of a

boarding house, where the Olivarez's and Fernando Hernandez were staying. It was located on Third Street, the farthest street west of the river. A friendly and hospitable husband and wife, assisted by their teenage son and daughter, operated the hotel. The building was two stories high with twelve guest rooms on the second floor. The first floor offered a large room as a restaurant serving meals to guests and citizens. In addition, a parlor for sitting or reading and a meeting room opposite the restaurant filled out the first floor. The kitchen had been built onto the back of the building and conveniently located through large, double doors at the rear of the dining room.

The hotel had a large porch which wrapped around its front and south sides with chairs and tables for the guests' comfort on warm evenings. A large, well-tended garden stretched out from the south porch for about 100 feet that ended beside a small road that led to the hotel stable. Walking paths wended their way through the garden and benches were placed strategically for folks to enjoy their walks. Giving the area a pleasant fragrance, many species of flowers were in full bloom.

The garden extended around to the rear of the hotel where the family had planted a variety of vegetables in neat rows. Behind the garden were several fruit trees including apple, cherry and peach. This family was obviously industrious and hard working.

James had seen Maria and her chaperone aunt in the garden. At the mention of Maria, William's heart began to race. Maria really was in St. Louis. *In the back of his mind had been fear that Maria might not be in St. Louis. He had expressed this to no one, as a silent sigh of relief escaped his lips. A vision of the beautiful and vivacious Maria filled his mind. He could see her dancing around the Tavern floor as he had seen her many months before in New Orleans.*

"William, are you with us?" James asked.

His three friends were looking at him as he forced the daydream out of his mind and brought his attention back to what James had been saying. He could see understanding on Jock's big, scarred face.

"Yes, please continue, James," stuttered William.

"As I said," James continued, "Maria and her aunt were in the garden. Maria was reading, and her aunt was working on some sewing. They did not see me. I went into the hotel and inquired about rooms as you asked me to, William. Two were available, so I took them signing the registration with my name. I explained that there would be four of us for several nights and horses that would need to be stabled. I paid for two nights in advance."

"You did well, James. Thank you." William said, now back in complete control.

"What did you learn, William?" Jeremiah asked.

"First, I went to the Federal Marshal's office to check on the Schmitts. They knew of Henry's escape from the Tennessee jail and of his sighting in Nashville but no more. His brother and uncle were last seen in the Alabama Territory over a month ago. None of the Schmitts have been seen in Missouri. Then, I went to the Bank of St. Louis to open an account for Maria with her mother's money and an account for us as business partners. Third, was my visit with the solicitor, recommended by Miss Olivia's attorney. I identified myself, and it turns out the solicitor is a friend of Jacob's who served with him in the Red Stick War. I showed him my papers, and he confirmed that they would stand up in court," William finished.

"What should we do now?" Jock asked.

"I would rather not go to the hotel until tonight for dinner. We might be seen and recognized. Jeremiah, however, would not be recognized. He could go to the hotel, stable our horses, and see what else he could learn," replied William.

"We three," William, indicating Jock and James, "could go to that public bath I saw on Second Street, wash this trail dirt off, and change into city clothes. Jeremiah can join us after he takes care of the horses. What time does the hotel serve dinner, James?"

"The owner said they serve starting at six o'clock," James replied.

"Good. I want to make our entrance after Maria and the others are seated in the dining room. Jeremiah, would you make sure we are all seated at the same table?"

A signal was arranged to let the three men know when to enter the restaurant. The men parted to meet later at the hotel at dinner time.

A bath would feel good. Clean clothes even better. The buckskin traveling clothes they wore were comfortable, but it was time to dress as city folk. After their bath, a walk around the city to get their bearings seemed in order. This city of more than 3,000 people exuded energy. It was exciting to be experiencing such enthusiasm.

The city boasted some famous residents including Captain Rogers Clark and Captain Meriwether Louis who explored the Missouri River and the Columbia River to the Pacific Ocean. Auguste Chouteau, the famous French explorer and founder of St. Louis, lived in the city and operated several businesses. He also exerted significant political influence within the city and territorial governments.

The three men, dressed in frock coats and britches, returned to the street where the Hernandez Trading Company was located. Jock wore his beloved silver-buckles on his shoes. Although silver buckles were no longer in style, that didn't matter to Jock. He loved them, and no one was going to say not to wear them to the giant man.

The men strolled by the Hernandez Trading Company and entered a nearby tavern. They ordered beer and listened to the talk that always existed in a tavern. Alcohol had a way of loosening men's tongues.

Jock pointed out the two men he talked with while they loaded one of the Hernandez wagons. As he did so, one of the men saw him.

"It's that big man who helped us load the wagon this morning."

Both men walked over to the table where William, Jock, and James were sitting.

"Sit down men," Jock invited, "We'll buy you a drink."

"Now that's right friendly of you, Jock. You're a good man."

"These are my friends William and James," Jock introduced.

The men sat down and after some light talk about the Trading company, William asked if the owner ever came in this tavern.

"Oh, no! This place would be beneath his royal highness. This is a working man's tavern," the first man answered; then he quickly continued, "Señor Hernandez works until about 5:30 pm then returns to the hotel for dinner with his fiancée. Señor Garcia, he leaves early and goes to one of those taverns on the water front. Those are dangerous places. There are fights and murders down there all the time. Those river men are a mean bunch, but I understand Señor Garcia has some friends down there."

William asked if Señor Garcia's first name was Manuel.

"Yes, do you know him?"

"I don't think so," was William's reply. "I thought he might be the Manuel Olivarez from New Orleans who was Señor Hernandez's business partner there."

"That's him. He goes by his Aunt's name here because of some trouble in New Orleans. Are you from New Orleans?"

William accepted this new piece of information, and his mind began working to put this puzzle together. *Maybe Manuel knew about the murders of old Ben and Sarah. Did he know of the capture of the murderers and William's escape? Did Manuel know his name? Was he expecting William to show up on his door step? And why didn't Fernando and Manuel drink together?*

"No, we're not from New Orleans, but we were there earlier this year and had occasion to learn about some of its residents. How do Señor Hernandez and Señor Garcia get along?" Jock innocently asked, mirroring William's thoughts.

"I don't think Señor Hernandez likes Señor Garcia but tolerates him," the second man commented.

"Señor Garcia's sister is Señor Hernandez's fiancée; otherwise, Señor Hernandez would throw him out, challenge him to a duel, and kill him," the first man chimed in. "One of these days Señor Hernandez is going to be pushed too far, and Señor Garcia will wish he had not talked back to Señor Hernandez so often."

"Señor Garcia is always getting money from Señor Hernandez, then gambling and losing. Señor Hernandez said yesterday that he would no longer pay off Señor Garcia's debts. Señor Garcia said, 'if Hernandez didn't pay, then he would lose Manuel's sister and Señor Garcia would tell about something that happened in New Orleans. It turned into a big fight in front of the men.'"

Subtly changing the subject, James asked some questions about the city and received some orientation instructions from the two men.

Enough time had passed. It was time to go watch for Jeremiah's signal.

William motioned to the waitress for another round

of drinks for the two men and laid some money on the table.

"We have a dinner engagement if you will pardon us." He stood and offered his hand to both men. "Thank you, for your company and conversation."

Out on the street Jock voiced the question William had been thinking, "Do you think Manuel knows the authorities are after him for the murders of Ben and Sarah, the capture of Ortega, and the killing of Chavez?"

"I don't know, but we better assume that he does," William replied. "The question going around in my head is: Does he know about Jock and me? We know if Miss Olivia wrote to her son, she would not have told him about us. But, Ortega might have told someone who could have written to Manuel."

"I wonder how much of this Hernandez knows?" James questioned. "I'll bet he doesn't know any of it."

"I'll bet you're right, James," Jock cut in. "Manuel doesn't want him to know anything of his unlawful affairs."

"Does this change your plans for tonight, William?" Jock asked.

"No, but we should keep a sharp eye on Manuel."

Chapter Thirty-One

Confrontation

Across the street from Maria's hotel, hidden in the growing shadows, William and his friends waited. They watched Manuel Garcia come down the street and enter the hotel. William's anxiety increased. *He was about to see Maria again and confront her brother and her fiancé. How would she react? What would she say and do? He needed to remain calm.*

Jeremiah appeared in a second floor window with a light. Finally, the signal.

Maria Olivarez, Elizabeth Garcia, Manuel Garcia and Fernando Hernandez descended the stairs and entered the dining room. Mrs. Blackburn ushered them to the large table near the windows. Fernando Hernandez objected, asking for a smaller four place table, but a quick glance around the room confirmed that no smaller tables were available. Reluctantly, he held a chair for Maria, then, seated himself next to her. Manuel helped his aunt with her chair, then, seated himself at the end of the table next to Fernando.

A tall, well-dressed young man entered the dining room and walked directly to the table where the four sat.

"Good evening, Señora Garcia, Señorita Olivarez, Señor Hernandez, and Señor Garcia," he said smiling; "I am Jeremiah Russell."

"Sir, we have never met," said Fernando indignantly. "How do you know us?"

"It is true we have never met, but I know a great deal about you, Señor," Jeremiah replied.

Before anyone could react further, another young man appeared at the table. As he took a seat next to Manuel, he said, "Good Evening, Señor Garcia, Señor Hernandez, Señora Garcia," then he looked straight into Maria's eyes and said, "Hello, Maria, it is nice to see you again."

Maria stared at him, a touch of fear showing on her face.

"How do you know my sister?" Manuel demanded.

"We met in New Orleans some months back. My name is James Woods."

As he finished speaking, a giant of a man walked to the table and stood behind the chair across from Aunt Elizabeth. "Good evening, Maria, you are as beautiful as ever. My name is Jock Smith, Señores and Señora. I am Maria's friend and Miss Olivia's friend. We met in New Orleans."

Maria's face held a look of confusion and fear, but she said nothing as if waiting for another shoe to fall. The chair opposite her was not yet occupied.

"You know our mother?" Manuel stammered, obviously unnerved and starting to rise.

Fernando was on his feet as a fourth young man came to the table and stood behind the chair opposite Maria. Looking directly at Fernando, he said "Please Señor Hernandez, be seated. We will explain our presence and purpose here. Then, if Maria wishes, we will leave you in peace."

Maria turned to Fernando, putting her hand on his arm, and softly said, "Please, Fernando, I do know these men. Let us hear what they want of us."

Grudgingly, Fernando sat down again, signs of anger showing on his face.

Manuel also slid back into his chair. But his face showed hatred as his eyes shot daggers at William.

William looked at Maria for the first time, and he knew how much he loved her.

"Maria, I am very happy to see you after so many months. Your mother sends you her very best regards. But I apologize, for I must bring you some very sad news, also."

Waiting for William to continue, Maria nodded, but she said nothing.

Then, looking directly at Aunt Elizabeth who had said nothing; however, as she was looking at him intensely, William said, "Señora Garcia, Miss Olivia sends you her fondest wishes for your happiness. We apologize for intruding on your evening meal."

"Thank you, Señor," replied Aunt Elizabeth.

William turned toward Manuel, "Your mother also has a message for you, and we will get to it in a moment."

"If you have a message for me from my mother, then give it to me and be gone," Manuel snapped in a loud angry voice, attracting the attention of some of the other diners.

"Please, Señor be patient. All will be made clear in a few minutes," responded William evenly, not raising his voice.

"My name is William Russell, and I am Maria's friend and, also, Miss Olivia's friend. We met in New Orleans in February." As William said his name, he was watching Manuel. A brief recognition passed over Manuel's face and was gone.

William sat down placing a leather case on the table. He removed some papers then set the case on the floor beside his chair.

"Sir, if this is business, my office would be a much more appropriate place to transact it," Fernando interrupted, looking at the papers.

"No, Señor Hernandez, this is not business. This is personal, and this is the right place for us to meet," William replied. He picked up a sealed envelope, "Maria, your mother has sent you a letter that will explain much about our reasons for being here." With that, he started to hand her the envelope.

Manuel's hand shot out, and he grabbed the envelop from William saying, "I'll take that. I'm Maria's guardian. She can't have anything I don't see first."

"That was very rude Manuel, but then you are not a very nice man. I expected you to react this way, so I offered Maria your mother's letter to you. Also, you are not Maria's legal guardian." William paused for this to sink in. "That responsibility has legally been assigned to someone else. Miss Olivia petitioned the New Orleans Court to change Maria's Guardianship, and this change was granted. Maria, I'm sorry to break this news to you so bluntly," William apologized.

"She cannot do that," Manuel almost shouted in his agitation. "I will have that changed immediately."

"Because you insist on being dealt with first, Manuel, we will do just that," William said. "You recognized my name when you heard it."

"You are the soldier," Manuel uttered, his voice dripping with hatred.

"Yes, and you are a very bad man. You tried to have me killed by your two hired thugs. They missed. Chavez was killed, and Ortega was caught. He confessed everything about your hiring them to hunt me down. They committed murder in your name to learn my whereabouts.

They were careless. They were seen and recognized. And they paid the ultimate price, but you know that already. Don't you? That is why you are using your aunt's name, not your own." William paused for effect.

With a decidedly unfriendly face, Fernando glared at Manuel.

Maria was staring at her brother in disbelief. "Manuel, how could you?" She demanded. Aunt Elizabeth held her hands to her face in a look of incredulity.

"Murders, what murders? They were just a couple of old slaves I owned. Killing a slave is not murder," Manuel said defensively.

"You are wrong. You did not own the slaves. Miss Olivia owned them, but she had given them their freedom. To kill free people of color is murder. And because you hired the men who committed the murders, you are complicit in the murders. That makes you a murderer," William explained. Then, turning to Maria, he softened his voice, "I'm very sorry to bring you such sad news. Old Ben and Sarah were killed by the men Manuel hired."

"Oh . . . No . . . It can't be," Maria cried, tears flowing from her eyes and down her cheeks, as she covered her face with her hands. Aunt Elizabeth put her arm around Maria's shoulders. With their heads together, they wept over the loss of two people they cared deeply about.

William turned back to Manuel who was watching the two women. He pulled a paper from the pile on the table and passed it across the table for Fernando, Maria, and Aunt Elizabeth to see. The "WANTED" poster had a picture of Manuel, his name, a reward of $500 dollars for his capture, and the authorization of the Federal Court of New Orleans. "The Federal Marshal knows you are here. They will be here to arrest you any minute. Your mother begs you to surrender and . . . ."

Manuel was out of his chair, running for the doors leading to the kitchen. James, Jeremiah, and Jock leapt after him. As Manuel reached the big double doors, Mrs. Blackburn came out carrying a large tray containing plates of food. Manuel grabbed the tray and threw it into Jeremiah's face. Manuel spun Mrs. Blackburn into James, who kept her from falling. Then Manuel rushed into the kitchen, overturning chairs and people in his mad charge-- anything to slow down his pursuers. The backdoor stood open to let the cooler evening breeze in. He ran through it, across the garden, and hurtled over the garden fence.

Jock came out the backdoor just in time to see Manuel disappear into the woods on the other side of the road. With James and Jeremiah right behind him, Jock entered the woods where Manuel had gone.

Once in the woods, Jock held up his hand for them to stop and listen. Sounds of someone running could be heard. Immediately, they started forward again, but the night was dark. Only the stars could be seen in the moonless sky. They stopped again to listen. The sounds were faint. Eventually, they knew that Manuel had gotten away, so Jock, James, and Jeremiah returned to the dining room.

Two men with badges were talking with William, Señor Hernandez, and one of the other diners when the three men came through the double doors from the kitchen.

"He got away," exclaimed Jeremiah in exasperation, as the men turned and looked at the returning pursuers.

"Don't worry, we'll catch him. We have a good idea where he is headed," one of the men with a badge offered. The two men turned and left the restaurant.

William introduced the other diner as Judge Breckenridge whom he had arranged to be present to observe the proceedings.

At that moment a good looking, well-built man, in

the blue and gold uniform of an Army officer, strode confidently into the dining room--turning every head. He went straight to William sticking out his hand. They shook hands and hugged, as they greeted each other warmly. Then, he greeted Jeremiah in the same way. The three brothers stood for a moment happy to be together again. Then, Jacob shook hands with James asking after his wound and his family. To Jock he gave a big smile expressing his pleasure at seeing him again and shook hands with Judge Breckenridge whom he knew. William introduced Jacob to Señor Hernandez; then he ushered Jacob to the table where Maria and Aunt Elizabeth were seated, observing the proceedings and trying to absorb the news about Ben and Sarah and the accusations against Manuel.

"It is my greatest pleasure to introduce my oldest brother Jacob," William announced to the women. "Jacob, this is Señorita Maria Olivarez and her Aunt Señora Elizabeth Garcia."

Jacob took Maria's extended hand saying, "You are every bit as beautiful as I have been told. I am very happy to meet William's friend." With that he bowed deeply and kissed her hand. Ever the charmer, he turned to Señora Garcia and took her hand. "How can you be a chaperone when you are so young and beautiful yourself," he bowed and kissed her hand, also.

Aunt Elizabeth blushed deeply at the compliment quickly producing a fan which she opened to move gracefully to and fro to deliver a cool breeze over her warm face.

Señor Hernandez came and stood beside Maria in a protective stance. He did not like Maria being the center of all this attention.

"If you are quite finished," he remarked to William, "We would like to eat our dinner in peace and alone."

"I'm sorry. Señor Hernandez, but we are not finished.

If we could all take our seats again I will continue," William responded.

Places were taken. A chair was brought for Judge Breckenridge. Jacob took Manuel's place next to Fernando.

William took several papers from the stack in front of him and passed them to the Judge.

The Judge read the pages, then confirmed: "These documents, signed by Señora Olivia Olivarez and verified by the New Orleans' Court Clerk, appoint Jock Smith and William Russell as legal guardians of her daughter Maria Olivarez to be applicable only until Maria returns to her mother's home. The papers also state that they will be responsible for her chaperone Señora Garcia."

"So, you are my guardian," Maria said, with an edge of anger. "Well, we will see about this. I suppose you are going to order me about like your servant. You want me to wash your clothes and cook your meals. I will not be your slave. Either of you," Maria's anger exploded.

"Whoa . . . wait a minute," William blurted, putting his hands up in protest.

"Nothing of the kind. We are not your dictators. Your mother only charged us with facilitating your safe return to New Orleans. That is provided that you wish to return to New Orleans. You are free to do whatever you wish. We have no hold on you. Your brother's dominance over you is gone. You have a mind of your own. You will make your own decisions. Jock and I are here to help you do whatever it is that you want to do."

"Sir, Maria is my fiancée. She is not free to do whatever she wishes," Fernando stated emphatically.

"I'm sorry, Señor Hernandez. Your engagement to Maria has been terminated by Maria's mother. Here is a letter to you from Miss Olivia stating that the promise of Maria's hand in marriage is broken. As the head of the Olivarez family, she has the right to break that promise.

Maria is no longer your fiancée. However, if she wishes to marry you, she may."

Señor Hernandez was on his feet. "Sir, you have insulted me in public. This is intolerable. I challenge you. If you win, Maria is yours. If I win, Maria is mine."

"Señor Hernandez, please calm down. I do not wish to fight you. In any case, Maria is her own person. She will make her own decision. Neither of us can win her by fighting a duel," William replied quietly.

"Are you a coward, Sir? Do you refuse the challenge?" Señor Hernandez said more calmly. He was experienced in making challenges.

"If we fight a duel, Señor, Maria's decisions will not be a part of it. If we fight, Señor, I will kill you." There was steel in William's voice that no one missed.

"My Seconds will call on you tomorrow. Come, Maria, we are leaving," Señor Hernandez stated, tugging at Maria's chair to pull it out for her.

Maria didn't move. She put her hand on her Aunt's arm before she could stand in response to Señor Hernandez's command to leave.

"I do not want either of you to fight a duel. That would be silly. There is no need. William is right; I will make my own decision. There is a lot for me to think about. Much has happened here tonight. I wish to be alone to think. I am going to my room. Aunt Elizabeth, please stay here and have your dinner. Please, ask Mrs. Blackburn to bring something to my room for me to eat. Fernando, please stay here and make peace with William. That is what I want you to do," Maria stood.

"I will not stay in the same room with this man," Señor Hernandez stated flatly, walking out of the room and out of the hotel into the night.

"Maria, before you leave," William gently added, "I have a letter for you from your mother. Please take it with you."

Maria took the envelope offered and left the room without another word.

Aunt Elizabeth started to follow Maria but was stopped by Jacob, who enticed her with, "Señora Garcia, please stay with us. Maria needs time to think, and I would like the opportunity to know you better. Look, here comes our food."

Mrs. Blackburn approached the table with a tray loaded with full plates.

"The last time I brought you men food, it ended up all over Mr. Russell there and my nice clean floor. If it happens again, you men will go hungry."

The meal was delicious. The men were hungry and every morsel disappeared quickly. Even William found he had a hardy appetite.

Chapter Thirty-Two

The Challenge

Deep in thought over last evening's events, William sat alone in the hotel restaurant, lingering over his morning cup of coffee. Jeremiah and James had left very early to visit the veterans' camp and to help with the building of the dugout canoes. Jock had left after breakfast on an errand for William. He had not seen Maria, Aunt Elizabeth, or Señor Hernandez yet this morning. Mrs. Blackburn had said that Señor Hernandez left very early in the morning, and the two women had eaten breakfast in their room.

A man entered the restaurant and walked directly up to William.

"Are you William Russell?" the man asked. Upon receiving an affirmative nod from William, he proceeded, "I represent Señor Fernando Hernandez who has challenged you to a duel in the matter of Señorita Olivarez. I am his Second. My name is Señor Michael Martinez. Is your Second available so that we may make arrangements for the duel?"

Showing his irritation, William let out a long sigh.

"I had hoped that Señor Hernandez would think better of this duel idea in the light of day and realize that it is a bad idea for us to fight."

"No, Sir. Señor Hernandez's honor has been deeply offended, and he demands satisfaction. However, if you apologize publicly and leave St. Louis never to see Señorita Olivarez again, he will consider his honor satisfied, and the duel need not take place. Do you accept these terms?"

Another exasperated sigh. "I do not wish to fight a duel with Señor Hernandez. Doesn't he realize a duel between us will cost him any chance with Señorita Olivarez?"

"Señorita Olivarez is promised to him as a wife. This is the Spanish tradition that cannot be changed. The promise was made. Your interference is totally unacceptable. You must leave or fight the duel. You have no other choice."

"There are always other choices, Señor Martinez," William responded. "The so-called promise of Señorita Olivarez was not made by the head of the Olivarez family. Her brother made the promise, and he did not have the authority to make it. The official and legal head of the Olivarez family, Miss Olivia Olivarez, revoked her son's promise. Señorita Olivarez is now free to decide whom she wishes to marry and when she wishes to marry."

"But this is simply not done," protested Señor Martinez. "The oldest male in the Spanish family is the head of the family. He alone can arrange marriages between families."

"That may be true in Spain, but this is America. It is not true here," replied William.

"Sir, if you will not cease this persistence that Señorita Olivarez is not promised to Señor Hernandez and leave St Louis, then you must meet him on the field of honor. I have arranged for Judge Breckenridge to officiate the duel; I have also arranged for a doctor and two witnesses to be present. The duel will take place on Bloody Island at 8:00 o'clock tomorrow morning. Señor Hernandez will provide pistols or swords whichever you would prefer."

William sighed, "You are determined for us to fight. Alright, if I must fight to insure Señorita Olivarez's freedom, then I will. I made a commitment to Miss Olivia to protect her daughter, and that is what I will do."

"Which weapon do you choose, Señor Russell, pistols or swords?"

"Neither, I choose bare knuckles."

"But Sir," Señor Martinez protested, "bare knuckles are not a dueling weapon between gentlemen. It is just not done."

"Very well then, I choose long rifles at 100 paces," William stated.

Again, Señor Martinez protested.

"Señor Hernandez challenged me, did he not? That means the choice of weapons is mine. Is that not true, Señor Martinez?" William said, standing. There was an edge of anger in his voice.

"You are pushing me into an unneeded fight. Since it seems there is no way out of this fight, then it will be fought on my terms or not at all. Do I make myself clear, Señor Martinez?"

"Perfectly. I will convey your remarks to Señor Hernandez," Señor Martinez replied, his voice, strained.

"I will be on Bloody Island with my Seconds tomorrow morning at 8:00 o'clock, and we will resolve this situation."

Without another word, Señor Martinez turned on his heel and marched from the hotel.

Furious that he had been forced into a duel, William sat down again. He did not want to fight Señor

Hernandez, but it seemed there was no other way to free Maria from him. He was deep in thought when a movement in the garden caught his attention. Maria and her aunt were walking to a bench near the fence.

When William entered the garden and advanced toward Maria, she was sitting next to Aunt Elizabeth. Maria stood, handed her book to her aunt, stepped forward extending her hands to him. William could see her big, beautiful smile that he remembered from their first meeting in the tavern and every time they were together after. Her black eyes twinkled with delight. She was the vision of beauty he had kept in his heart. A huge lump rose in his throat, as he was filled with emotion, hoping his smile reflected hers.

He took her extended hands in his, and paused to take in this vision of loveliness. He wanted to remember every detail. "You are absolutely gorgeous," he stammered.

She laughed. "You flatter me, Sir. Now, you must tell me everything from our last meeting until this very minute, how you met my mother and old Ben and Sarah."

At the mention of Ben and Sarah, a sad look crossed her face. She led him by the hand to another bench a few feet away. Aunt Elizabeth did not follow. Before sitting next to Maria, William turned to Aunt Elizabeth, bowed, and said "Good Morning."

"My mother's letter explained a lot, but I still have many questions."

William took his time describing his hunt for Maria in New Orleans, his return to the city with Jock to find her, their meeting Ben and Sarah and her mother, and finally, learning of the men her brother had hired to kill him. He covered every detail. He even told her a little of his conflict with the Schmitts, and the wounding of his father. When he finished and she had exhausted all of her questions, the sun had risen to directly overhead. Aunt Elizabeth had listened from her seat a few feet away. She also asked several questions particularly about Señor Hernandez and his involvement with Manuel's plots.

At this Maria told him of her brother's discovery of her *unchaperoned* meeting with a soldier in the park and dancing in a tavern. Someone had seen them and reported this to Manuel. He had been absolutely furious, and he forbade her from ever seeing the soldier again and from ever leaving the house without a chaperone. Manuel's anger had frightened her so that she sent Sarah to warn William and to break off their friendship.

When William had seen her on the balcony and yelled and waved, Manuel's fury had gone deep and silent. When Señor Hernandez left for a business appointment, he confronted Maria in front of Aunt Elizabeth. His cold anger almost out of control, he slapped Maria very hard, knocking her backward into Aunt Elizabeth who kept her from falling. Shouting if the soldier returned to the city house to find her, Manuel left, swearing to kill the soldier. Manuel said he would return in an hour and would take care of the soldier so that Maria would never see him again.

Aunt Elizabeth and Maria immediately ordered Ben to get the carriage and drive them to the plantation. They had decided the sooner Maria was away from New Orleans, the safer the soldier would be.

Mrs. Blackburn interrupted them when she came to the porch and asked if they would like lunch. She said she would fix them a fruit drink and some sandwiches they could have in the garden if they wished to stay where it was cooler. The day was quite warm and muggy as July days in Missouri tended to be.

Jock and Blue Bell drove up to the barn just as Mrs. Blackburn's daughter brought a large tray and pitcher. One look at Jock as he entered the garden, she chuckled and thought aloud she had better bring another tray. Everyone smiled at this idea--even Jock who pleasantly agreed with her.

A slight breeze helped keep the garden comfortable while they enjoyed the food. True to her word, Mrs. Blackburn's daughter brought another tray.

"Jock, were you able to learn anything about the steamboat anchored in the river?" William asked.

"Yes," replied Jock, "it sails for New Orleans in two days. We can get a small cabin for Maria and Aunt Elizabeth, but you and I must sleep on deck with the crew and work as deck hands. If these arrangements are agreeable to everyone, I can return to the captain this afternoon and make the final arrangements."

"Maria, there is something else that I must tell you." William interjected, "Señor Hernandez will not withdraw his challenge. He is determined that we must fight a duel over you. If he wins, you are to be his wife immediately, and I am to drop all efforts for your freedom to choose whomever you want. I have conveyed to him that those terms are unacceptable to me and to you. Your freedom from your brother's arranged marriage is now legally and permanently established, and he cannot change it no matter what duel he wants to fight. Perhaps you could talk to him and persuade him to drop this unnecessary duel. Unless, of course, you want to marry him," William held his breath at this last option, afraid she might want to marry Señor Hernandez.

Maria was quiet for a long time. Knowing she was deep in thought, no one spoke.

Finally, she answered, "I do not want to marry Fernando. He is so much older than I. He is not the bad man as so many people think. I do wish to return to New Orleans as soon as possible. My mother will help me decide where I go and what I do with my life now that I have the freedom you say I have. I do not want you and Fernando to fight a duel. My heart would be broken if either of you were hurt. I will send Fernando a note requesting that he come to see me."

"I offered to fight this duel with bare knuckles. The first one knocked off his feet would lose. That way neither of us would get hurt. The fight would be for his honor only nothing else. I don't know whether or not he has accepted these terms. If you can talk him out of the duel, it would be better for everyone involved. This fight is not necessary," William replied.

"Jock," Maria said, "I will be very happy if you will make the final arrangements for our return to New Orleans on the steamboat. Aunt Elizabeth and I will begin immediately to prepare to leave."

"I will go with Jock," William indicated. "We will return for supper."

The men found the captain of the steamboat supervising the loading of the cargo bound for New Orleans and other ports along the river. They made a quick trip to the bank and the fares were paid. The captain was relieved because he had all space sold, plus two additional crew members. William and Jock were satisfied that they could fulfill their promise to Miss Olivia to escort her daughter home.

When William and Jock entered the hotel, Maria was waiting for them. "Fernando refused to read my letter," she told them. "He had stated to the messenger that he would not return to the hotel until after the duel, that he would talk with me after you, William, were removed from my life and only then. He is being so stubborn it infuriates me. You must get him to read my letter before the duel. Once he reads my letter, I do not think he will wish to continue with the duel." She handed William the letter in a sealed envelope.

"If he won't read it, I'll read it to him," William promised. "Don't worry; there will be no fight."

Chapter Thirty-Three

Bloody Island

The bow of the rowboat slid onto the sand of Bloody Island's riverside beach next to the other three boats that had been pulled up there. Smoking and talking, three boatmen sat in the shade of a scrub tree. Jock had rowed the hired boat across the river with the ease of an experienced sailor.

Brushing the sand from the seat of his pants, one of the boatmen stood up.

"You're the last. Now, the duel can begin. Just follow that path," he said, indicating a well-worn footpath into the heavy underbrush.

The five men picked up their weapons from the bottom of their boat.

"Wow . . . you came loaded for bear." One of the boatmen exclaimed as the men, rifles in hand, started for the footpath. The boatmen got up to follow at a distance.

William knew Señor Hernandez would drop the challenge once he read Maria's letter, so he was in good spirits. Jeremiah and Jacob, William's brothers, Jock, and

James all felt there would be no duel. This exercise was just an errand they had to go through to ensure Maria's freedom.

The men were dressed in their buckskin traveling clothes and moccasins, except for Jacob who wore the plain uniform for daily wear. None of the men wore hats.

"You know, James," Jacob said, "You and William look enough alike with your sandy brown hair and hunting jackets to be brothers."

James walked beside William, "Yes, but I have brown eyes and he has blue. Now, as I was saying, my father and I caught this fish on the Tennessee river just off an island like this. It was one big catfish."

As they passed a large tree, James stepped ahead of William and Jacob then turned to face them, holding his hands apart to show the size of the fish.

Three rifles exploded in the brush at the side of the path ahead of them. James' body froze for a couple of seconds, then crumpled to the ground. Shot in the back, he never knew what hit him. He was dead before he fell.

William's reaction was almost too slow as twigs and leaves splattered over him. Two more shots had come through the foliage of the tree beside him where he had been an instant before. The others had dropped to the ground when the first shots were fired. William looked back just in time to see Jock crawl into the brush followed by Jeremiah.

Keeping low, Jacob came up beside William. "Are you alright, William?" he asked.

There were shouts coming from down the path, and someone was running toward them.

"Who's shooting? What is going on? Good Lord, someone's been shot!"

William could see Judge Breckenridge and Señor Fernandez come into view about 200 hundred feet away, followed by a third man William did not know.

"Stay back!" Jacob shouted. "There's been an ambush and killing. The killers are hiding in the brush. Stay where you are."

The men stopped and ducked behind a clump of stunted-growth trees at the side of the path. They were not armed.

William found an opening in the underbrush beneath the tree. He crawled forward on his stomach pulling James' rifle, as well as his own, with him. Jacob, with his pistol drawn, followed. To his left William saw Jeremiah raise his rifle and fire. The explosion was immediately followed by the sickening sound of a lead ball striking flesh. A shout of pain came from somewhere in the bushes ahead. It was followed by a stream of curses. William knew the voice. It was Henry Schmitt.

A rifle ball shattered the branches where the smoke from Jeremiah's rifle lingered. Jeremiah was no longer there. In Indian fashion, he had moved as soon as he had fired. Reloading his rifle, he was now several feet away hidden behind a tree.

William figured Jock to be on Jeremiah's left near the river bank although William could not see him. Suddenly, a rifle exploded near the river. Jock had fired. Several yards in front of William, a black-clad figure stood up clutching his midsection, then pitched forward over the bush he had been hiding behind, and fell motionless to the ground. William could not see who had been shot. Two shots aimed at Jock's position rattled through the bushes where he had been. There was no sound from Jock.

This narrow island could not be a worse place for an ambush. There was little room to maneuver. Dense brush as high as a man's waist covered much of the sunlit areas, but under and around the trees the bushes thinned out or didn't grow at all. In those places someone lying on the ground could see as much as fifty feet. Any movement might be seen. William moved only his eyes to search the terrain in front of him. Any change in his position might bring a bullet slamming into him. The enemy was close at hand, so he determined a quick shot would be better than taking time to aim.

The leaves on the tops of the bushes, where the black-clad man had fallen, waved unnaturally in the still morning air. Someone was crawling in the brush. William fired through the bush. An arm flew up then disappeared. William rolled to his left immediately after pulling the trigger. A lead ball dug into the ground where he had been lying. Jacob fired, a grunt and a gasp then no further sound. Henry let out a stream of curses vowing to kill all Russells. He was still in the fight and dangerous.

Quiet settled over the island. Even the birds were silent. Henry stopped cursing. William waited not moving. Jacob was perfectly still beside him. A movement could cause a giveaway sound that would let the enemy know where to shoot. Patience was needed now. They would wait for the enemy to make the next move.

Minutes passed. Muffled sounds of whispering came from the people on the path. Señor Hernandez, the Judge, and the other man had gone to where James' lifeless body fell. William could not hear what was being said.

As William lay waiting, his thoughts turned to James. *He had spoiled the first shots of the Schmitts by suddenly stepping in front of William and Jacob. He had saved their lives and given his own. William felt a great sadness at the loss of his friend and at the same time a great anger at those who did this thing. There had been three shots by the ambushers, followed by two more. Did that mean there were five ambushers? He had to assume there were five. Henry was wounded but possibly still able to shoot. The black-clad figure that Jock had shot, lay motionless near the river bank. No sound or movement came from the man whose arm had reflexively raised when he was*

247

shot. The man who grunted when Jacob shot remained quiet also. Could he be wounded and still ready to fight? Most likely, he was still in the fight because a shot had been returned toward Jacob. Two maybe three of the ambushers were out there ready to kill.

"This is Judge Breckenridge," the judge shouted from the path. "You men stop this shooting. Put down you weapons and come out. There will be no more killing. We can settle this peaceably. Come out and surrender," he demanded. "Do you hear me? Come out now!"

"Judge," Jacob said, just loud enough for him to hear. "There are two or three of the ambushers just waiting for us to show ourselves. If we come out, we will be shot."

To confirm Jacob's answer, a shot punctuated the stillness. The rifle ball splintered the bark of the tree that concealed him.

A hush fell over the island again. Then, just audible, William and Jacob could hear movement in the brush directly in front of them. Someone was trying to run in the dense undergrowth. The sounds revealed him to be headed for the men on the path. William crawled forward. When the footpath came into view, he drew himself into a crouching position behind a low scrub tree. A shot whipped through the branches above his head, splattering debris over him. This shot was followed by a rifle shot from Jeremiah. They heard a scream of pain.

William turned toward the footpath. Señor Hernandez stood looking toward a man running into the brush on the east side of the path. He turned to William.

"That was Manuel. He is running for the Illinois side."

Did Manuel have a gun? William wondered. *He was not carrying a rifle when he ran into the brush.* William slowed. He did not want to charge into a pistol shot. He turned and entered the brush several yards from the point where Manuel had entered. Señor Hernandez was right behind him. William stopped to listen. Manuel was still running through the brush; then, that sound ended, and the noise of splashing water could be heard.

When William and Señor Hernandez reached the river bank, they could see Manuel waist deep in the river wading toward Illinois. The river was not more than sixty feet wide at this point, and Manuel had about reached the middle. The current didn't appear to be very strong.

"Manuel, come back. You cannot get away," Señor Hernandez shouted. "Give yourself up, and I will help you."

Manuel turned his head and looked back at Señor Hernandez.

"I cannot. They will hang me." He continued trying to reach the other side. He stopped, twisted his body to see Fernando.

"Help, I am in quicksand." He started trying to free himself by splashing and flailing about. He was panicking.

Two of the boatmen appeared at the end of the island.

"He is stuck in quicksand," William shouted. "Go get your boat and pull him out."

The men ran for their boat on the other side of the island.

"Quit struggling, Manuel," Señor Hernandez yelled at the panicked man. "You only make it worse."

Manuel sunk deeper. His waist was now below the water. William searched the banks of the island for anything that could be used to help the struggling man. A driftwood log, probably from some cabin, lay on the bank a few feet from him.

"Fernando, if we can get that log into the water, we might be able to float it out far enough for Manuel to grab and pull himself free." William yelled.

The two men ran to the log and began to try to roll it toward the water. It was very heavy. They couldn't budge

Gene House

it. Just then Jock came out of the brush behind them. He sized up the situation in a glance and immediately began to help roll the log. With Jock's help, the log rolled to the water's edge, then into the water. But the water was too shallow for the log to float. Manuel was still struggling with every ounce of energy he could muster. Señor Hernandez continued to shout at him to stop moving and be still so he would not sink any deeper. Now, only Manuel's head and shoulders could be seen.

The three men maneuvered the log farther into the river, and the log began to float. William, keeping downstream from the log, pushed its smaller end out into the river and pointed it toward Manuel. Fernando supported the middle of the log, and Jock anchored the end nearest the shore. The current was faster than they had first thought, making it difficult to keep the log floating toward Manuel. The men stayed downstream of the log and kept it turned perpendicular to the current. By wading backwards, they moved the log toward Manuel who was still better than twenty-five feet away.

A row boat rounded the end of the island. The two men in the boat were pulling hard toward Manuel who was now up to his neck in the water. Manuel was screaming and beating the water. He could not see the three men with the log edging deeper into the river, but he could see the boat headed for him. William, who was now waist deep in the river, was closest to Manuel when he felt his feet sink into the muck on the river bottom.

"I'm in the quicksand," he yelled, turning toward Señor Hernandez and Jock who were holding the log to keep it perpendicular to the current. William put his arms over the log resting his chest on the top of it and started working to free his feet.

A powerful hand grabbed William's wrist and began pulling him and the log back toward the bank. Señor

250

Hernandez had William, and Jock had Señor Hernandez's other hand. They were pulling him free. First, his left foot came free of the muck, then his right foot. By pulling William out of the quicksand, they lost control of the log. Señor Hernandez helped William stand. The log turned in the river current, missing Manuel by ten feet.

Only Manuel's face and forearms could be seen above the water, but the boat was close. Then his face slipped beneath the water, his arms continued their frantic movements for a moment, then disappeared. The boat arrived. One of the men fished under the water for a few minutes and found Manuel's lifeless body. They put a rope under his arms and slowly pulled him to the surface and into the boat.

William, Señor Hernandez, and Jock watched from the river bank. They had tried, but it had not been enough. Silently, they returned to the footpath. Judge Breckenridge with Jacob and Jeremiah waited beside James' body. Someone had covered James with a blanket. Three other men, including Señor Martinez, were there. Henry Schmitt was lying beside the path barely alive. There was blood all over his midsection. He had been gut shot. Next to Henry sat his cousin, the Nashville deputy, with a bandage around his left thigh and one around his right arm.

One of the men picked up a medical bag and said, "Mr. Smith, let me look at your side. That wound needs attention."

William swiftly turned to his friend, concern showing on his face. A large blood-soaked area covered the left side of Jock's hunting jacket.

"Do not ye worry, William. It is only a flesh wound. The ball just took some of that extra fat I've been putting on since I've been eating your mother's and Mary's cooking," he joked.

From the deputy, they learned that he and Henry had

met their uncle and Henry's brother, Beau, in St. Louis. They had planned to go west where none of them were wanted. They heard that Manuel Olivarez was looking for some men to kill an enemy who had poisoned his benefactor against him. Needing traveling money, the Schmitts had located Manuel.

Manuel had offered them a hundred dollars for the killing. When the Schmitts learned it was William Russell that the Spaniard wanted killed, their enthusiasm grew. When they learned his brother, Jeremiah, was with him, the Schmitts agreed to kill both of them. But Manuel wanted the big man, Jock Smith, killed as well. The Schmitts agreed, but it cost Manuel another hundred. Manuel told them of the duel and wanted the killing done before the duel to protect Señor Hernandez.

Bloody Island, where the duel was to take place, would be ideal for their purpose. Manuel had intended not to go with the Schmitts, but they insisted he join them and take part in the killing. They had stolen a boat and rowed to the island the previous night. That boat they pulled into the bushes on the Illinois side of the island where no one would see it.

The men looked at each other. Ironically, there had been a boat they could have used to save Manuel--if they had only seen it. There was a sick feeling in the pit of each man's stomach. Manuel probably thought he would not be able to get the boat into the water before he got caught, so he tried to wade across the river.

William pulled Maria's letter from his breast pocket. Luckily, it had not gotten wet. He handed it to Fernando who walked a few feet up the path to read alone. When he finished, he stood for a long time with his arms at his sides. Then he walked to William.

"There will be no duel. Maria has rejected me as a suitor and as a husband. She wishes to return to New Orleans. I love her very much, and it hurts to lose her."

"She will always be your friend, Señor Hernandez. When you sell your business and return to New Orleans, I'm sure she will want to see you," William replied.

"You love Maria, also," Señor Hernandez stated. "Do you plan to marry her?"

"I will marry her if she will have me, but she will make up her own mind about that." William had a knot of uncertainty in his throat that he did not want to show.

The Judge and doctor wanted Henry and the deputy to be taken to St. Louis for further treatment and jail. The authorities would have to retrieve the bodies of Manuel and the Schmitts. The Russells and Jock would take care of James' body. Very carefully, James was carried to the boat. Silently, Jock rowed them to the Levee. William and Jock stayed with their friend while Jeremiah and Jacob made arrangements for the funeral and burial.

James was buried in the St. Louis cemetery. William and Jock bought a stone to mark the grave. Maria, Aunt Elizabeth, and Señor Hernandez attended the funeral.

Henry Schmitt passed away before they could load him into a boat. The city of St. Louis would not take the two Schmitt bodies, so they were buried on Bloody Island in unmarked graves.

Señor Hernandez arranged for Manuel's body to be buried in St. Louis. William and Jock accompanied Maria and Aunt Elizabeth to Manuel's burial. Señor Martinez and several business acquaintances also attended the service.

Chapter Thirty-Four

New Beginnings

The small group of people gathered on the Levee at 8:00 am to board the steamboat for the trip to New Orleans. William and Jock shook hands with the two older Russell brothers.

"Will you look after Blue Belle for me, Jacob?" Jock asked.

"You can be sure of that. I have arranged for all of your horses to be boarded with a farmer friend of mine," Jacob replied, smiling. "Don't worry. They will be fine until you return."

"Jeremiah, you be careful going up the Missouri. It's a treacherous river. Find Jock and me a good piece of land, too," requested William.

"I will do just that," Jeremiah responded.

Maria stood in front of Señor Hernandez. "You will come see us when you return to New Orleans?" She smiled and kissed him lightly on the cheek. then she turned and boarded the steamboat with William and Jock.

Aunt Elizabeth stepped in front of Señor Hernandez.

She took his hands in hers and said, "You are a good man, Fernando. You are very important to me. I look forward to your calling on me as soon as you return home." She hugged him.

"I will come call on you in New Orleans," he replied, a little surprised at her boldness.

She hugged him again then boarded the steamboat and stood next to Maria. The screech of the boat's steam whistle started the big stern paddlewheel pulling the boat out into the river. When the boat reached clear water, it turned south.

Three weeks later the boat reached New Orleans. As soon as the passengers were disembarked with their luggage, William hired a carriage for the ride to the plantation.

Miss Olivia was sitting on her porch when the carriage turned into the lane that led to her front steps. She stood and walked to the front of the porch.

Maria jumped out of the slowing carriage and ran to her mother before the carriage stopped. The family reunion was accented by tears, and laughter, and excited chatter. Sam came from the barn and was warmly greeted by Maria, Aunt Elizabeth, William, and Jock. Even Sadie came out for a greeting.

Miss Olivia extended her hands to William and Jock. "You brought my little girl home. Thank you, so very much. I knew you would."

The sad news was saved for later.

That afternoon Miss Olivia would ask about her son and Señor Hernandez. Tears flooded her eyes as William told of Manuel's plot and death. Maria put her arm around her mother's shoulders as she cried over his misspent life and unnecessary death.

That evening at dinner Miss Olivia offered William the position of overseer of the plantation at a very good wage. If he and Maria were to get married, he would become its owner. A very good proposal indeed.

The next day Maria found William sitting alone on the porch. She sat beside him and held his hand.

"You and Jock have done so much for me and my family; we can never thank you enough," she began. "I know you love me and want to marry me. I like you very much William, but I do not love you."

William felt weak. His head spun. He hurt all over. He could say nothing as she continued.

"You are a wonderful friend, and I will always treasure our friendship. I know I am hurting you now, but the truth is best no matter how much it hurts. I want to go to Spain and become a dancer and entertainer like my mother. My aunts and uncles in Spain will help me. They have connections with the academies. My mother has written to them, and they look forward to my arrival in Spain." Maria's enthusiasm for her adventure was contagious even to William, in spite of the pain he felt.

Maria excitedly talked about her trip to Spain sailing across the ocean, meeting family she had only heard about, and the training in dance she would receive.

William's concentration on Maria's new adventure lagged behind her declarations of her plans. His mind tried to deal with the disappointment and the pain he felt because of his one-sided love for her. It hurt too much to continue to dwell on those feelings.

Another thought forced its way into his consciousness, a thought that had been plaguing him ever since Bloody Island. *This thought increased his melancholy. His lifelong, best friend had died taking the shots meant for him. He knew that telling the Woods' family of James' death would wound them very deeply.*

Returning home would be sad and difficult because of the news he brought, but he knew his family would be relieved and happy to have him home again.

A final reflection jumped into his consciousness.

William knew that Martha, James' sister, liked him, probably even loved him. She had said as much when William left the Woods' farm to go to St. Louis. William wondered. *How would she feel now, knowing her brother, James, had saved his life?*

And how did he really feel about her? He had known her all his life. They had grown up together. He had always enjoyed being around her and joining with her caring for the animals around the farm and in the forests. But, mostly he had thought of her as a friend who was fun and who liked to do many things he liked to do. However, . . . in their last few meetings, he had begun to notice she had grown into a beautiful, young woman. Would their friendship mature into mutual admiration, respect, and love?

Appendix

The Spanish Dancer novel is a work of fiction set in the historic year of 1815. All of the characters in the novel are fictitious with the exception of Rachel Jackson, Andrew Jackson's wife. The words that I put into her mouth could easily have been said to soldiers who fought under General Jackson if they stopped at his home, the Hermitage, to pay their respects to the general. Because the story takes place during and after the War of 1812, there are references to some famous persons of the time, but they are not characters in the story.

My great, great grandfather, Andrew Russell, was a six-month enlistee in a Tennessee Volunteer Regiment. He saw service in the Alabama territory. He was not at the Battle of New Orleans, and, as far as I know, he did not participate in any major battle. However, while researching his genealogy, the idea for the novel occurred to me. The Russell name has been used for the main character, William, to honor Andrew's service.

The history books that discuss the battle of New Orleans on January 8, 1815, do not always agree on the numbers of casualties on both the British and the American sides. I have chosen to use the account by Charles B. Brooks, (1961), *The Siege of New Orleans* for the casualty estimates in my story. The average private in General Jackson's Army probably never heard the exact casualty figures. A private would be lucky to hear much more than "the British lost a lot of men, maybe over 2000, and we didn't get hurt bad at all, only a few dead."

On New Year's Day, according to Brooks, the British bombarded the American positions knocking out several canons including a 32-pounder, a 24-pounder and a 12-pounder. When the British ran out of ammunition, Major General Edward Pakenham stopped the attack.

The beginning of the battle of New Orleans is described by Charles B. Brooks, (1961), *The Siege of New Orleans*, p. 252, and Robin Reilly, (1974), *The British at the Gates – the New Orleans Campaign in the War of 1812*, New York, Putnam, p. 297. These accounts helped me describe the conditions my characters experienced early in the morning the day of the battle. Reilly remarked, "On January 8, 1815, the British attacked in the darkness of early dawn and in a heavy fog. When the British soldiers began to approach the American line, light filled the eastern sky."

The Americans had built defensive earthworks, including cotton bales, on the side of the Rodriquez Canal. David Saville Muzzey wrote in *A History of Our Country*, p. 193, a brief description of Jackson's hastily built defensive line. This position was called "Line Jackson."

The breaching of the earthworks by a British charge is depicted in the painting *Battle of New Orleans* by Herbert Morton Stoops and is mentioned in *War of 1812*, at gatewayno.com/history/war1812, without any detail other than the Americans drove the British back. I chose to fictionalize a breach for my characters.

The death of the British commander, Major General Pakenham, during the battle is widely reported in every account of the battle that my research unearthed. I believe that the Americans would have learned of this very quickly after the battle, and the news would have spread throughout the Army. The deaths of the other three high-ranking British commanders would also have been learned quickly by the Americans. The *Union 1812,* by A. J. Langguth, discusses how devastating the loss of these high-ranking commanders was to the British. Those fatalities were significant in the decision by the British to quit the battle and retreat.

Also, A. J. Langguth and others describe General Jackson, after the battle ended, seeing dead British soldiers rise up and surrender to the Americans. Hundreds of soldiers had been playing dead. Langguth suggests over 500.

These losses plus the continuous pressure by Jackson on the remaining British forces pushed them to board their ships and sail away.

The British did not return to England after their defeat at New Orleans. Instead they sailed to Mobile Bay, Alabama Territory, and attacked and captured Fort Bowyer. That was the last battle of the war where American forces fought the British Army. This news probably reached General Jackson's headquarters in New Orleans well before the Tennessee regiments started for home.

The news of the Treaty of Ghent ending the war, which had been signed before the battle, did not reach General Jackson until several weeks after the battle, according to the *Union 1812* by A. J. Langguth. The Treaty of Ghent signed on December 24, 1814, and taking effect February 18, 1815, ended the fighting. The terms of the treaty stated that the fighting between America and Britain would cease immediately. The United States Senate promptly ratified the treaty.

The disbursement of various units in General Jackson's Army is my fictitious interpretation of how each brigade and regiment was sent home. The history books in my research only stated that the Army had been disbanded after the battle. The few regular troops in Jackson's Army remained in New Orleans.

Jean Lafitte's biography *Gentlemen Pirate of New Orleans*, by Joseph Geringer, noted that for his support of the Americans at the Battle of New Orleans, he and any of his men who fought for the Americans would receive a pardon for their pirate activities. This clemency by General Jackson, I employed for the character Jock Smith. Lafitte's biography also describes his base of operations on the island of Baritaria in Baritaria Bay.

The online history of the *General Land Office* provided the bounty land information. For my story, I merged that online history information and the actual experience of my great, great grandfather, Andrew Russell, to bring bounty land payments to veterans.

In May 1812, an act of Congress was passed which set aside bounty lands as payment to volunteer soldiers. Land was set aside in western territories that became part of the present states of Arkansas, Michigan and Illinois. This land was acquired by veterans through a multi-step process beginning with the issuance of bounty land warrants. Veterans applied for and, if granted, used these warrants to apply to the General Land Office for land. However, lands in Missouri were later substituted for those in Michigan, due to a report by the Surveyor General who quite misleadingly described, as undesirable, the land in Michigan that had been set aside for bounty land. Other later acts of Congress, until 1855, continued to address needs of soldiers wishing to redeem their bounty land warrants.

John Gardiner was appointed Chief Clerk of the General Land Office in 1812. A map of the northern part of the Missouri Territory, prepared under his direction, shows the proposed bounty lands in Missouri. This is perhaps the earliest printed map of the Missouri Territory and perhaps the first map to show the progress of township surveys west of the Mississippi River. The Missouri map shows the locations of the proposed bounty lands for the veterans of the War of 1812, primarily North of the Missouri River and West of the Mississippi.

Barry Lawrence Ruderman, Antique Maps, Inc., provides a copy of the map, dated Washington 1818, by mapmaker John Gardiner. Among the more noteworthy events attributed to Gardiner was his removal of the General Land Office records from Washington, by carriage, during the siege by the British. His name appears on several early maps, including maps of the bounty lands in the Illinois Territory.

For instance, a private with six months' service would receive 80 acres, as the US Government prescribed. However, the Bounty Land was not authorized by Congress until 1840. On a personal note, a copy of the Certification granting my relative Andrew Russell 80 acres, and other documents stating these facts, are in his file in the Family Archives and in the *Liberty, Missouri, Archive & Historical Library*. The bounty lands given to Continental Army soldiers for their service in the Revolutionary War were primarily in Ohio, Kentucky, Virginia, and Tennessee.

Concerning my inclusion of a "sulky" being used by Jock Smith, I have chosen the one described by the *Encarta Dictionary*: English (North America) defines a sulky as a "light open two-wheeled vehicle for one person, pulled by one horse." The seat was attached to springs bolted to the sulky frame. The driver's feet would be braced against a strong crossbar. Sulkies had been used for racing as early as 1790. The sulky became popular as a means of transportation soon after. I decided to use the sulky in my story because it was different, and it could be modified.

According to J. Percy Hart's *History of the Three Towns; Bridgewater, Brownsville and West Brownsville*, the first steamboat, the *Enterprise*, to travel from Pittsburgh, Pennsylvania, to New Orleans did so in 1814. The first steamboat built in Bridgewater was begun in 1811 and launched in December of that year into the Monongahela River.

While I found a reference in the *Wikipedia Encyclopedia* to steamboats visiting St. Louis in the early 1800s, it is inconceivable to me that those early steamboats did not make St. Louis a regular port-of-call. I, therefore, incorporated this idea into my story. The top speed of these early boats was estimated to be about five miles-per-hour. This speed I used to estimate the sailing time from St. Louis to New Orleans.

Louisiana's history describes its early settlers of Baton Rouge, in the mid-1700s, as French-speaking Canadians driven into exile by British forces during the French and Indian war. These exiles, popularly known as Cajuns, are descendants of Acadia in Canada's maritime region. At the time of my story, Baton Rouge was an unincorporated settlement.

My descriptions of St. Louis in 1815 are taken from the *St. Louis City Plan Commission -1969, Physical Growth of the City of St. Louis, A History of St. Louis* which describes the town's growth from its founding through the 1800s. Also, *Breckenridge's Views of Louisiana*, for 1811 describe St. Louis as a town "built between the river to a second bluff with three streets parallel to the river and a number of other cross streets at right angles." At that time, St. Louis was the seat of the territorial government. It had been incorporated by the Court of Common Pleas in 1809 and covered an area of 7.63 square miles. Its population was estimated to be about 1200.

Bloody Island in the Mississippi River was a sandbar

Gene House

island opposite St. Louis, which became densely wooded and a rendezvous for duelists because it was considered neutral and not under either Missouri or Illinois control. The Island first appeared (perhaps from delta silt?) in 1798. It grew continually and eventually became part of Illinois by attaching itself to Illinois in the late 1800s. At the time of my story, duels on the Island occurred occasionally, thus the name, Bloody Island. *The State of Missouri, History of Duels* describes several famous duels that occurred on the island.

Concerning the long rifles used by my characters William Russell and James Woods, they were sometimes called the Kentucky rifle. According to descriptions by the *Kentucky Rifle Association*, this rifle was used by early Americans both civilians and military. It has an unusually long barrel thought to have been a unique development of the American rifle makers. The rifle became popular in 1732 and remained in use by the American military until 1850. It had a flintlock action and was accurate from 82/250 yards, sometimes longer in a skilled marksman's hands.

The musket used by Jock Smith was a smooth-bore long gun, primarily the weapon of choice of the British Army in both the Revolutionary War and the War of 1812. The musket's range of accuracy reached 50 to 70 yards. During the War of 1812 the fourth regiment of the United States infantry carried muskets to defend the ramparts of Baltimore when the Star-Spangled Banner was written. Don Troiani stated this in his *History of the 4th Regiment, 1812*. The 1795 US infantry musket had a .69 caliber and 44 ¾ inch long, round barrel.

A pirate's cutlass is described in the online history of weapons, as a weapon used for close-in fighting and more to scare than to kill. The range in size of the cutlass is from 18 inches to 36 inches long. This information may be found at thepiratesrealm.com website.

About the Author

After a 40-year business career in Kansas City, New York City, and Tempe, Arizona, **Gene House** retired in the desert Southwest. With time to pursue other interests he began writing the history of his family. It was while writing the biographies of family members that he discovered the joy of writing.

The novel *The Spanish Dancer* germinated when he wrote about an ancestor who fought in the War of 1812. Early American history has always fascinated him. The lives of the early settlers of Tennessee and the Missouri Territory have become favorite subjects. Many of his short stories were written in that genre.

His writing accomplishments include: *Adventures along the Dash*, an autobiography and memoir, *House Family, Ancestors and Descendants*, plus several articles and essays. Every day he spends several hours in front of the computer, writing or researching a story–except during football season.

Gene, also, has become an avid landscape water colorist and has illustrated some of his children's stories and memoirs.